THE CONTROL OF NAVAL ARMAMENTS

BARRY M. BLECHMAN

THE CONTROL OF NAVAL ARMAMENTS

Prospects and Possibilities

THE BROOKINGS INSTITUTION
Washington, D.C.

Library of Congress Cataloging in Publication Data:
Blechman, Barry M
 The control of naval armaments.
 (Studies in defense policy)
 Includes bibliographical references.
 1. Disarmament. 2. United States. Navy.
3. Russia (1923– U.S.S.R.). Voenno—Morskoi Flot.
I. Title. II. Series.
JX1974.B475   327'.174   75-5153
ISBN 0-8157-0987-7 pbk.

9 8 7 6 5 4 3 2 1

THE BROOKINGS INSTITUTION is an independent organization devoted to nonpartisan research, education, and publication in economics, government, foreign policy, and the social sciences generally. Its principal purposes are to aid in the development of sound public policies and to promote public understanding of issues of national importance.

The Institution was founded on December 8, 1927, to merge the activities of the Institute for Government Research, founded in 1916, the Institute of Economics, founded in 1922, and the Robert Brookings Graduate School of Economics and Government, founded in 1924.

The board of Trustees is responsible for the general administration of the Institution, while the immediate direction of the policies, program, and staff is vested in the President, assisted by an advisory committee of the officers and staff. The by-laws of the Institution state, "It is the function of the Trustees to make possible the conduct of scientific research, and publication, under the most favorable conditions, and to safeguard the independence of the research staff in the pursuit of their studies and in the publication of the results of such studies. It is not a part of their function to determine, control, or influence the conduct of particular investigations or the conclusions reached."

The President bears final responsibility for the decision to publish a manuscript as a Brookings book or staff paper. In reaching his judgment on the competence, accuracy, and objectivity of each study, the President is advised by the director of the appropriate research program and weighs the views of a panel of expert outside readers who report to him in confidence on the quality of the work. Publication of a work signifies that it is deemed to be a competent treatment worthy of public consideration; such publication does not imply endorsement of conclusions or recommendations contained in the study.

The Institution maintains its position of neutrality on issues of public policy in order to safeguard the intellectual freedom of the staff. Hence interpretations or conclusions in Brookings publications should be understood to be solely those of the author or authors and should not be attributed to the Institution, to its trustees, officers, or other staff members, or to the organizations that support its research.

FOREWORD

The United States and the Soviet Union are now discussing two major arms control issues—the limitation of strategic arms and the reduction of forces in Europe. A successful outcome of either negotiation would reduce the risk of military confrontation between the superpowers and promote general political stability. A third source of possible conflict—naval competition—has received scant attention, however. The United States and the Soviet Union both use their navies to express diplomatic intent in times of crisis, to support allies, counter threats, and deter intervention by third powers. Their fleets sometimes confront one another in politically charged situations and, with surface vessels vulnerable to surprise attack, the risk of conflict is always present.

The size and capabilities of the two navies are therefore significant indicators of national resolve. And any change in relative military strength is interpreted by third nations to signify that the United States or the Soviet Union is more or less willing to commit itself to an active role in world affairs. Thus naval competition exacerbates a tense political climate; it encourages a greater global rivalry between the superpowers and may aggravate regional and local crises.

Barry M. Blechman's intent in this volume, the ninth of the Brookings Studies in Defense Policy series, is to stimulate public discussion of the naval arms control issue. He reviews previous attempts to control navies through negotiation, describes alternative approaches, and outlines several specific proposals. Examining each aspect of the issue from the perspectives of the United States, the Soviet Union, and interested third powers, he concludes that the most promising approach to naval arms control would be to strive for either of two kinds of agreement: one that would establish ceilings on number and tonnage of warships in three separate categories, or one that would limit the size and duration of naval deployment in the

Indian Ocean. He warns, however, that any naval arms control agreement implies complicated tradeoffs between risks and benefits that need to be shrewdly assessed in the context of contemporary international politics.

Barry M. Blechman is a senior fellow in the Brookings Foreign Policy Studies program. The Institution thanks Philip A. Odeen, George H. Quester, General Matthew B. Ridgway, Henry S. Rowen, and R. James Woolsey—members of its Defense Advisory Board—for their helpful comments. Others who gave generously of their time to comment on the paper include Robert M. Behr, Robert J. Murray, Major General W. Y. Smith, Rear Admiral Harry D. Train II, and Vice Admiral Stansfield Turner. The author would like to thank his Brooking colleagues, Philip J. Farley, Edward R. Fried, Henry Owen, Jeffrey Record, and Alton H. Quanbeck, for their suggestions. He is also grateful to Captain Charles D. Allen, Jr., N. Bradford Dismukes, Jerome H. Kahan, Anne M. Kelly, Lieutenant Commander Jerry A. Kotchka, Michael K. MccGwire, James M. McConnell, Norman Polmar, Commander Gary Sick, Commander Nepier V. Smith, and Robert G. Weinland for their advice. Barbara P. Haskins edited the manuscript. It was typed by Ruby M. Roberts. Research assistance was provided by Louisa Thoron and Stephanie Levinson.

The Institution also acknowledges the assistance of the Ford Foundation, whose grant helps to support its defense and foreign policy studies. Nevertheless, the views expressed here are those of the author alone, and should not be ascribed to those who commented on the study, to the Ford Foundation, or to the trustees, officers, or other staff members of the Brookings Institution.

KERMIT GORDON
President

January 1975
Washington, D.C.

CONTENTS

Tables

CHAPTER ONE

INTRODUCTION

Navies have long been the handmaidens of diplomacy. A nation's navy not only defends its coastal waters and protects national interests abroad; it also signals overall military potential and political intent to influence world affairs. Changes in relative naval strength among the leading powers have always been watched closely in other nations on the assumption that the size of a country's conventional naval forces reflects its willingness—and ability—to affect political events. This assumption prevails even today when more potent weapons are available.

Navies support diplomacy in more direct ways as well. Armed confrontation between opposing fleets has often marked the opening of hostilities between great powers; perhaps just as often it has led to a settlement of their dispute. And great powers frequently have relied upon warships to impose their will upon lesser states. There is even a special term for this: gunboat diplomacy.

Superpower Naval Competition

These political uses of navies have survived, indeed have flourished, in the nuclear age. Since the Berlin crisis of 1961, nearly every confrontation between the superpowers has featured sizable naval deployments: the Cuban missile crisis (1962), the Middle East Six-Day War (1967), the face-off near North Korea after the destruction of an American reconnaissance aircraft (1969), the Jordanian civil war (1970), the conflict over Bangladesh between India and Pakistan (1971), the fourth Arab-Israeli war (1973), and several lesser incidents. In each of these crises the threat of actual combat between the superpowers was implicit as opposing fleets faced one another in regions

1

of high political tension; in some there were dramatic incidents when one or other had to back off from an announced or tacitly implied action.

The use of naval forces during crises is very easy to understand. Warships are more mobile, more flexible, less disruptive in an economic, political, and psychological sense, and often more visible than other forms of conventional military power. Compared to strategic nuclear weapons, they imply less risk of a mutually disastrous war, at least in the short run. Thus the United States and the Soviet Union maintain fleets in several regions of the world to indicate their commitment to various states in the areas. At times of rising tension both powers tend to reinforce such deployments and to move warships closer to the trouble spot so as to demonstrate concern for their respective allies, bolster the client's confidence, warn off potential adversaries, or carry out specific military tasks. Ordering warships away from the danger zone, sending them into port, or a similar move often signals lessened tension.[1]

Even during rare tension-free periods superpower rivalry is often expressed in relative naval force strength. Using such a comparative measure to indicate superpower foreign policy intent has a more complicated rationale than the obvious reason for crisis deployments. After all, strategic nuclear weapons provide the United States and the Soviet Union with such enormous potential destructive power that warships brandishing conventional armaments appear somewhat inconsequential. Perhaps the continuing focus on naval forces is a carryover from those days when the capital ship was *the* strategic weapon of the great powers. But a more important consideration is likely to be the general assumption that precisely because the destructive potential of nuclear weapons is so awesome, any decision to use these weapons would be irrational or a desperate final gamble by an international actor facing a major disaster. And, if nuclear weapons are unlikely to be used, then it is the superpowers' relatively conventional military capabilities that will determine the outcome of hostile interactions. The question of naval balance is therefore still a key issue in international affairs and compe-

---

1. Contrasting interpretations of the political efficacy of naval forces during crises are presented in Edward N. Luttwak, *The Political Uses of Seapower* (The Johns Hopkins University Press, 1974); and George H. Quester, "Naval Arms Races: Functional or Symbolic?" in Quester (ed.), *Seapower in the Seventies* (Dunellen, forthcoming).

tition in naval armaments a real and important element in the continuing rivalry between the United States and the Soviet Union.

The argument then follows that if relations between the two superpowers are to continue to improve, they must at some point begin to
discuss means of controlling naval competition. Yet naval forces are
used for specific national purposes that have little to do with U.S.–Soviet
rivalry. These functions might be affected adversely by a superpower
naval arms control agreement. There are potential risks as well as benefits associated with any measure of naval arms control: risks for the nation's security in the short term and in the long term, risks for the flexibility of U.S. foreign policy and the degree to which policy could be
supported by military force, risks that affect U.S. relations with its allies
and other nations. Before the United States can endorse any specific proposal for naval arms limitation, it must evaluate the substance of the
proposal within the context of prevailing international politics.

Types of Control

Any form of limitation on naval armaments is likely to be selective.
The U.S. and Soviet Navies each support national interests that have
little to do with superpower rivalry. In fact, mutual competition often
distorts these countries' views of national interest and can, consequently,
waste both nations' resources or be needlessly risky, maybe acting as a
catalyst for major conflict. Negotiated measures of naval arms control
offer the prospect of at least reducing these aspects of competition and
thereby international political tension. Of course, whatever is gained
through negotiation depends on the type of agreement that is attained.
Broadly speaking, there are two classes of agreements on naval arms
control.

Limits on Naval Inventories

One class of agreement, limits on naval inventories, would attempt
to control the number, type, or characteristics of warships maintained
by the signatories. Devising agreements of this sort is the delight of
military analysts and arms control specialists, for possible approaches
are numerous and complex. Agreements can focus on various indexes of

naval capability: the number of ships, tonnage, firepower, manpower, expenditures, and the like. They can be comprehensive, covering all types of vessels, or restricted to specific kinds of ships or even certain kinds of weapons on board ships. They can be simple or complicated. And they can approach the subject in either a positive or negative way; that is, they can specify a certain ceiling on naval armaments or demand a certain reduction to existing forces.

In the most simple form of naval inventory limitation, the United States and the Soviet Union may agree to restrict the overall number of ships in their navies, but it is doubtful that a satisfactory agreement can be reached based solely on such an aggregate limit. More complicated agreements will probably be necessary because a "ship" is not a rigorous or necessarily a homogeneous unit of measurement. An agreement that restricts only the total number of ships in each inventory would equate thirty-year-old U.S. destroyers with brand-new Soviet cruisers. Or, for that matter, it would specify an equal tradeoff between the Russian 800-ton *Nanuchka*-class missile corvette and the American 90,000-ton nuclear-powered *Nimitz*-class aircraft carrier. Thus an inventory limitation agreement might preferably address ships in several categories individually, each category representing different age, type, and size groupings. But even a more sophisticated agreement such as this, which would be more difficult to negotiate, still does not resolve problems arising from qualitative differences in the armament, ship design, propulsion, or electronic systems of the two navies.

In addition to promoting certain foreign and domestic policies (discussed later in this paper), agreements to limit naval inventories may also help to reduce defense costs for both the United States and the Soviet Union. Naval expenditures are beginning to increase rapidly in the United States. Aside from pay and price rises, much of this increase is due to the major shipbuilding and weapons modernization program begun in the late 1960s. Announced plans for further modernization imply continuing real increases in U.S. naval expenditures. A conservative estimate based on current plans shows an average real annual increase of 4 percent in obligational authority for naval forces between fiscal 1975 and 1980.[2]

The budget appropriation item, Shipbuilding and Conversion (SCN),

2. Barry M. Blechman, Edward M. Gramlich, and Robert W. Hartman, *Setting National Priorities: The 1975 Budget* (Brookings Institution, 1974), p. 97; see also pp. 84–88, 95–98.

may indicate more spectacular growth. At the extreme, if force levels are not permitted to decline further, modernization of U.S. naval forces could result in SCN appropriations averaging more than $6 billion a year between fiscal 1976 and 1980. After accounting for price increases, this would represent a rise of about 80 percent from the SCN average for the 1971–75 period, and more than 130 percent from the average for the 1966–70 period.[3]

Data on Soviet military expenditures are not available, but it is thought that Soviet naval expenses are lower than those in the United States. Estimates of what it would cost in the United States to acquire and operate a force of the same size and composition as the Soviet Navy range from about one-third to slightly more than one-half the annual cost of the U.S. Navy. It is unclear whether Soviet naval costs are rising as quickly as those in the United States, but if its current shipbuilding program is any indication, Soviet costs have been relatively steady since about 1968, leading one to believe that their naval expenditures may be relatively fixed.[4] The director of the Central Intelligence Agency, William E. Colby, estimated recently that overall Soviet defense expenditures had risen about 3 percent a year since 1960. There is no evidence that the rate of growth in naval spending has exceeded this figure.[5]

Nonetheless, if an agreement to limit naval inventories helped to reduce defense spending, this could have an important effect on Soviet decisions, despite this lower level of expenditure. Measured by gross national product, available resources in the USSR are roughly half those of the United States[6] so that the defense burden on the Soviet economy is considerably greater than that on the U.S. economy. A reduction in

3. SCN figures for fiscal years 1966–75 are from *The Budget of the United States Government—Appendix*, relevant years; SCN figures for 1976–80 are author's estimates. Price increases for the period 1966–75 are assumed to follow the average rate for defense purchases; price increases from 1976 to 1980 are assumed to average 8 percent a year.

4. Michael K. MccGwire, "Current Soviet Warship Construction and Naval Weapons Development," in Michael K. MccGwire, Kenneth Boothe, and John McDonnell (eds.), in *Soviet Naval Policy: Objectives and Constraints* (Praeger, 1975), pp. 424–51.

5. Statement by William E. Colby in *Allocation of Resources in the Soviet Union and China*, Hearings before the Subcommittee on Priorities and Economy in Government of the Joint Economic Committee (1974), 93 Cong. 2 sess., pp. 32–33.

6. *International Economic Report of the President Together with the Annual Report of the Council on International Economic Policy*, February 1974, p. 91.

the shipbuilding program could free rubles for consumer products or for investment to spur Soviet economic growth. For that matter, they could be used to expand activities in other military sectors.

Of course, the extent of potential savings depends strictly on the agreement. The first round of the strategic arms limitation talks in 1972 (SALT I) demonstrated that too much should not be expected of initial agreements. They are not likely to bring about major reductions in defense spending. However, in the second or third rounds—over the longer term—agreements might bring about sizable reductions in force levels and consequently in naval budgets. Moreover, the political atmosphere might then be much more conducive to unilateral reductions beyond those envisioned by the agreement itself. On the other hand, it might lead to greater spending, lending support to arguments for rapid modernization and against those favoring unilateral reductions in force levels—the choice between the two possibilities depending mainly on the domestic political consensus at the time.

Limits on Naval Deployments

The second broad class of naval arms control agreements limits naval deployments by partially regulating the operations of naval vessels. Signatories to an agreement of this sort are permitted to build and maintain any number of naval vessels of any type. There are constraints though on the specific regions in which some or all of these ships can operate. Measures of this nature have been reached in the past, particularly during the interwar period, but with a mixed—generally poor—record of success. This approach is attractive from some points of view, however, and new arrangements have been suggested frequently in recent years.

Such limitations on naval deployments can take several forms. The most far-reaching measures bar the deployment of naval forces in certain regions completely. Since World War II, the Mediterranean, Caribbean and Baltic seas, Indian Ocean, and various portions of the Atlantic and Pacific have all been proposed as likely candidates for such an arrangement. Less ambitious proposals have been suggested prohibiting only certain kinds of naval forces such as submarines, or, even more narrowly, submarines carrying strategic missiles.[7] The purpose of a

7. The suggestions regarding submarines carrying strategic missiles preclude a signatory from operating within missile range of another signatory's territory or sphere of influence, a limitation that is becoming less useful as the range of sea-

similar type of proposal is to "denuclearize" an ocean area; that is, prohibit the deployment of ships carrying nuclear weapons and possibly those that are nuclear-propelled as well. The aim of another arrangement is to reduce, rather than eliminate, the naval presence in a certain zone. This type of agreement places negotiated limits on the number or tonnage of ships that can be deployed to a region at any time and, possibly, on the length of time that individual vessels can remain there. Such restrictions were included in the Montreux convention with respect to naval deployments by nonlittoral states in the Black Sea and apparently continue to operate effectively today.[8] These kinds of restraints, of course, can also be applied only to certain kinds of ships.

Although the superpowers may be able to avoid incremental expenditures for naval programs if naval deployments are limited in this fashion, it is not an effective way to reduce the cost of defense. These agreements can be easily and almost instantly abrogated, unlike controls on naval inventories that can only be violated over a period of years—however long is required to build modern warships. Moreover, some forms of limitation on naval deployments would be difficult to enforce or verify; controls on submarines would be one example, denuclearization agreements would be another. For these reasons, each signatory to such an agreement would probably opt to maintain, at least for the near term, its current force levels at the time of signing. These forces, operating in a region close to the one subject to the restrictions, would provide a hedge against a sudden violation of the agreement.

Benefits derived from this type of agreement relate mainly to the military risks of naval competition. The proximity of potentially hostile navies in certain regions invites confrontation. At times when international tension runs high, and military conflict seems imminent, there is considerable pressure for one side or the other to conduct a preemptive

---

based ballistic missiles grows longer. Conversely, more recent suggestions regarding the control of such submarine deployments have tended to stress maintaining them *within* certain regions. These proposals define preserves within which antisubmarine forces are to be barred, and in which, therefore, the submarines can be secure from attack. See Kosta Tsipis, Ann H. Cahn, and Bernard T. Feld (eds.), *The Future of the Sea-Based Deterrent* (M.I.T. Press, 1973).

8. Convention Regarding the Regime of the Straits with Protocol Signed at Montreux, signed July 30, 1936, by Australia, Canada, France, India, Irish Free State, Italy, Japan, New Zealand, Union of South Africa, United Kingdom, and United States of America. For text, see *Index of British Treaties* (London: Her Majesty's Stationery Office, 1970), p. 849.

disarming attack. Surface navies particularly, but also submarines, are sufficiently vulnerable to a first strike that the outcome of a naval engagement could well depend upon the timing of the initial attack. Thus, removing these naval forces could help reduce incentives for a first strike. Thereby, it could reduce both the risk of war due to accidents or overly aggressive local commanders, and the probability of conflicts resulting from a miscalculation by one of the superpowers as to the other's intent.

Potential Risks

Any form of arms control involves risks as well as benefits—risks for the nation's security, risks for the flexibility of foreign policy and the degree to which policy initiatives could be supported by military force, risks with regard to relations with allies and other states.

Of particular importance to the United States is the danger that an agreement designed to improve relations with the Soviet Union might affect relations with other states in an adverse fashion. The needs of the two superpowers for naval forces are not symmetrical, and these needs are not determined exclusively, or even primarily, by considerations of the rival's naval power. The United States is more dependent upon alliances with powerful overseas industrial areas—Western Europe and Japan—than the Soviet Union. Since the Second World War, public opinion in the United States has generally supported the view that the nation's security can best be ensured by a strategy of forward defense— the maintenance of a series of military alliances, formal and informal, with various nations around the world. These alliances are based primarily on U.S. defense commitments made credible by the presence of U.S. military forces in the regions. While Western Europe and Japan are the most significant members of the alliance system, others—notably Israel and Korea—are also recipients of U.S. commitments guaranteed by the presence (or proximity) of U.S. military forces. In some regions, particularly the Mediterranean and the Western Pacific, naval forces are the most visible symbol of these U.S. guarantees. Naval arms control agreements may cause allied states to doubt the intentions of the United States. For any specific agreement, this risk of eroding confidence by U.S. allies needs to be weighed carefully against potential benefits.

The Soviet Union also views its Navy as a useful instrument to support foreign policies relatively divorced from its relations with the United States. Soviet naval deployments in the Pacific and the Indian Ocean may be motivated primarily by perceptions of defense requirements vis-à-vis the People's Republic of China. And like the United States, the USSR finds its naval forces effective in incendiary situations developing within the third world.

Other potential risks are associated with specific types of agreements and are examined in later chapters.

Purpose of this Study

Although current prospects for naval arms control agreements appear slight, this should not deter either the public or government officials from considering new initiatives.[9] It has been demonstrated convincingly in recent years that unexpected events in the international political arena have a habit of changing convictions about what is or is not possible with remarkable rapidity. The aim of this paper is to provide a starting point for such a process.

This paper first reviews the benefits and risks entailed in certain types of proposals to limit naval inventories. It then discusses proposals to limit naval deployments. Lessons are drawn from history that are relevant to the design of future agreements, specific arrangements are described, and each one is evaluated from the perspectives of the United States, the Soviet Union, and interested third parties. Although an evaluation of each agreement is presented in the concluding section, the

---

9. My pessimism stems from two considerations. First, the superpowers are already engaged in two major arms control negotiations—the strategic arms limitation talks and the discussions regarding force reductions in Europe. These major diplomatic undertakings limit the attention that key government officials can pay to new initiatives. Moreover, while the talks continue, civilian leadership in the nations concerned may be reluctant to raise the prospect of new controls on their armed forces for domestic reasons. Second, the momentum of détente, apparent since 1969, has slackened during the past two years. This trend partly reflects the influence of domestic factions on both sides hostile to détente; it is evident in the reluctance of both nations to make certain key concessions. The Middle East war in October 1973 further eroded mutual confidence and set back the prospects for cooperative measures to restrain military forces. In barely managing to avoid a direct confrontation in the Mediterranean, the United States and the Soviet Union gave practical proof of how little they are willing to cooperate and the consequent fragility of détente.

objective of the paper is not to persuade. Rather, its intent is to illuminate the complexity of the tradeoffs between the risks and benefits implied by any potential agreement and thereby to assist readers to reach their own conclusions as to the desirability or undesirability of proposals.

It should be noted that the types of arrangements discussed in this paper concern only the general purpose navies of the superpowers. A third broad class of agreements—those that either limit strategic naval systems or the antisubmarine warfare forces that threaten those systems—are not considered here. Similarly, multilateral agreements that include limits on navies other than those of the superpowers are not reviewed. These omissions are not meant to prejudge the potential usefulness of such arrangements.

CHAPTER TWO

LIMITATIONS ON NAVAL INVENTORIES

Understanding the problems of limiting superpower naval armaments requires, first of all, at least a cursory familiarity with the overall size, composition, characteristics, and operating patterns of the navies of the United States and the Soviet Union. Such a review is presented in appendix A. It compares the two forces in 1974 and, also more tentatively, what they will look like in 1980.[1] Any measure of arms control will take time to negotiate and has to be related to projected rather than present circumstances.

Comparison of the Two Fleets

The outstanding feature about the two fleets is how much they differ from each other.

From the end of the Second World War through the mid-sixties, U.S. naval planning concentrated on the development of sea-based forces for

---

1. Discussion in appendix A has to be brief. For further information regarding the Soviet Navy, the reader is referred to Michael K. MccGwire, Kenneth Boothe, and John McDonnell (eds.), *Soviet Naval Policy: Objectives and Constraints* (Praeger, 1975); Michael K. MccGwire (ed.), *Soviet Naval Developments: Capabilities and Context* (Praeger, 1973); and Barry M. Blechman, *The Changing Soviet Navy* (Brookings Institution, 1973). The annual posture statements of the secretary of defense and the chairman of the Joint Chiefs of Staff, and testimony of other Defense Department officials before the Armed Services and Appropriations Committees of both houses of Congress are the best sources regarding the present capabilities and future plans for the U.S. Navy. Also, comprehensive surveys of the force levels and characteristics of all the navies of the world are given in: John E. Moore (ed.), *Jane's Fighting Ships* (Sampson Low, annual editions) and Jean Labayle-Couhat and Henri Le Masson (eds.), *Flottes de Combat* (Editions Maritimes et d'Outre-Mer [EMOM], biannual editions).

the projection of U.S. power abroad—so that U.S. ground forces in Europe or East Asia could be supported during conflict, and so that other forces would be immediately available in strength to meet emergencies elsewhere. Thus the heart of the 1974 American fleet still consists of aircraft carriers—whose main purpose is the projection of air power ashore—amphibious assault forces, escort ships to defend projection forces, and related support vessels. In the late sixties, however, the increase in Soviet naval capabilities, U.S. experience in Southeast Asia, and other international and domestic political events brought about a gradual restructuring of American naval priorities. This new naval doctrine stresses "sea control"—the United States must establish and maintain naval dominance in particular ocean sectors so as to ensure access to those regions. The development and acquisition of attack submarines and various detection and weapon systems against airborne, surface-ship, and submarine attack are now uppermost in naval planning. This new thrust is likely to be reflected in the structure, composition, and capabilities of the U.S. Navy in the late 1970s and the 1980s. The change is not immediately apparent, however, because most naval vessels are multifunctional. Rather, it is indicated by trends in the allocation of research and development funds, the design characteristics of new ships and component subsystems, and the new naval doctrine. For example, aircraft carriers are useful both for projection and sea control missions; but the types of aircraft that typically constitute a carrier's air wing might well differ in accord with the relative importance given to each mission.

Unlike the United States, the Soviet Union did not emphasize the acquisition and global deployment of surface warships. Since the 1950s, the Soviet Navy's strongest components have been a huge fleet of attack submarines and a land-based air arm chiefly composed of reconnaissance and strike aircraft. In more recent years, the Russians have begun to deploy a force of modern surface warships, ranging in size from corvettes to small aircraft carriers. Combined with other developments, this indicates a gradual change in Soviet naval doctrine. Whereas in the past the Soviet Navy was designed and operated primarily as a defensive force—to deter and if necessary to defend the Soviet homeland from attack from the seas—the modern Soviet Navy seems to be assuming a wider range of roles. The most important include deployment of strategic nuclear weapons, deterrence of Western sea-based interventions on the periphery of the USSR (for example, in the Middle East), and carrying out various peacetime missions, such as show-the-flag cruises and other military demonstrations. In general, the Soviet Navy is changing from a force reserved only for wartime contingencies to one used to support Soviet foreign policy in peacetime.[2]

Thus aside from differences in the performance characteristics of their ships, weapons, aircraft, and electronic systems, and aside from differences in their respective numbers of ships of different kinds, the U.S. and Soviet Navies differ in an even more fundamental sense—in the relative priorities each accords to the potential roles of seapower; indeed, in the importance of seapower itself. These divergences are not accidental; they reflect the two states' different geographic positions; perceptions of their global role and how different kinds of military force should support that role; dissimilar histories; how much each is willing to use its resources to develop its respective naval capabilities; and many other contrasting ideas and experiences. Whatever the cause of these differences, however, and although mission priorities seem to be slowly converging, one consequence is to make it very difficult to compare the two fleets—and, therefore, even more difficult to negotiate agreements to limit fleet size and its various components.

Nonetheless, this problem is not insurmountable if the two sides have the political will to reach agreement. Some historical precedents may show ways in which this can be done.

Previous International Agreements[3]

Three agreements concluded during the interwar period provide interesting insights into the risks, benefits, and determining conditions if limits are to be set for naval inventories.

2. A series of monthly articles in the Soviet *Naval Digest* by the Soviet commander-in-chief, Admiral S. G. Gorshkov, argues forcefully for these newer missions. See S. G. Gorshkov, "Navies in War and Peace," *Morskoi Sbornik* (February 1972–February 1973). Interpretations of the Gorshkov series can be seen in Robert G. Weinland, Michael K. MccGwire, and James M. McConnell, "Admiral Gorshkov on 'Navies in War and Peace,' " Research Contribution 257 (Arlington, Va.: Center for Naval Analyses, 1974).
3. This section was prepared with the assistance of Louisa Thoron.

Greek-Turkish Protocol of 1930

In 1930, Greece and Turkey appended a protocol on naval armaments to a treaty of neutrality, conciliation, and arbitration.[4] In this document, the two states pledged that they would give each other six months' notice before acquiring additional naval vessels. The effect of the protocol was to forestall a threatened expansion in the number and type of warships deployed in the Aegean Sea. The agreement seems to have been effective for most of the 1930s. And when the two states did begin to expand their fleets toward the end of the decade because of increasing tension in the Mediterranean and more generally in Europe, they continued to keep one another informed and attempted to maintain some sort of equilibrium in the Aegean.

In effect, the Greek-Turkish protocol indicates that it is possible to achieve one of the objectives of naval arms control—stabilization of the naval balance between two countries in a shifting political climate— without actually negotiating specific limits on force levels or warship characteristics. In this case, at least, mutual statements of intent and frequent consultation served to control an incipient arms race. However, the agreement was of tenuous duration and dependent upon the continuing goodwill of both parties. It also hinged on the fact that the states concerned were relatively satisfied with the existing naval balance.

Washington and London Naval Treaties of 1922 and 1930

Until the United States and the Soviet Union signed the strategic arms limitation agreements in 1972, the Washington and London naval treaties of 1922 and 1930, respectively, constituted the only serious attempt in modern times to limit the development and deployment of weapons central to the military posture of the great powers. The treaties are impressive in the scope of their objectives, in their elaborate and prudent detail, and in their efforts to take account of the conflicting interests of five independent parties in several interrelated but relatively autonomous arenas. Most historians agree that they had an important effect on naval expenditures during the interwar years and, consequently, on how fast

4. Treaty of Neutrality, Conciliation, and Arbitration between Greece and Turkey, with Protocol Respecting Limitation of Naval Armaments, signed April 1930, at Ankara, by Greece and Turkey.

and in what way the navies expanded. Yet despite this to their credit, the overall evaluation of the treaties is still dubious. Many observers question how they affected the balance of military power and—what is more important—their long-run effect on political relations among the great powers.[5]

The treaties dealt individually with distinct ship types—capital ships (battleships and battle cruisers), aircraft carriers, heavy cruisers, light cruisers, destroyers, and submarines—but they were far from comprehensive. Ship type, with the obvious exceptions of aircraft carriers and submarines, was defined by a combination of size (the tonnage range of vessels in a particular category) and armament (the caliber range of guns on ships in that category). For example, heavy cruisers were defined as ships the diameter of whose guns ranged between 6.1 inches and 8.0 inches, and which did not exceed a displacement of 10,000 tons. The Washington treaty was concerned almost exclusively with capital ships and aircraft carriers. The London treaty extended controls to the other ship types, but only for three of the signatories (the United States, Great Britain, and Japan). France and Italy never acceded to these later provisions. Noncombatant vessels, mine warfare ships, and small combatant vessels were never limited.

The primary means used to index naval capability in the treaties was aggregate tonnage. Signatories were permitted to maintain an inventory of ships of each type whose aggregate tonnage did not exceed a specified ceiling. For example, the United States and Britain were each permitted to maintain capital ships whose standard displacement totaled

5. Treaty between the United States of America, the British Empire, France, Italy, and Japan, signed 1922 at Washington, D.C.; Treaty for the Limitation and Reduction of Naval Armament, signed 1930 at London by the same signatories. (See *Index of British Treaties* [London: Her Majesty's Stationery Office, 1970], pp. 636 and 757, respectively.) There is a large body of literature devoted to accounts and analyses of these arms control agreements. The following might be of particular interest to the reader: Richard Dean Burns and others, *Disarmament in Perspective: An Analysis of Selected Arms Control and Disarmament Agreements between the World Wars, 1919–1939,* A study prepared by the California State College at the Los Angeles Foundation for the Arms Control and Disarmament Agency, ACDA/RS-55 (Los Angeles: ACDA, 1968). An interesting analogy between the naval treaties and contemporary strategic arms limitation is drawn in Hedley Bull, *Strategic Arms Limitation: The Precedent of the Washington and London Naval Treaties* (University of Chicago, Center for Policy Study, 1971). The text of the treaties is also given in "Multi-lateral, 1918–1930," vol. 2 of Charles I. Bevans (ed.), *Treaties and Other International Agreements of the United States of America, 1776–1949* (U.S. Department of State, 1969).

525,000 tons; Japan, 315,000 tons; and France and Italy, 175,000 tons apiece. The ratio of tonnages in capital ships approximated 5 : 5 : 3 : 1.8 : 1.8 (for the United States, Great Britain, Japan, France, and Italy, respectively); but it differed from these norms for the other ship types.[6] Generally, the rule was to ensure parity between the United States and Britain, and between France and Italy. Sizable differentials were demanded between all other pairs of signatories.

The tonnage ceilings were objectives that could be attained only after a certain period of time. When the Washington treaty was signed the actual size of the signatories' fleets was somewhat different from that allowed. The treaty was quite detailed in its provisions governing choices as to which ships were to be destroyed, the manner in which they were to be rendered nonoperable, and which vessels then under construction could be completed so as to reach the specified limit. The treaties also included limits on modernization rates: capital ships and aircraft carriers were to be replaced only after they reached twenty years of age, and there was to be a ten-year moratorium on the construction of new capital ships (later extended to fifteen years). There were three other important points. First, the treaties left it up to each state to monitor compliance of the other signatories; there were no provisions for on-site inspection. Second, they included collateral restraints on land facilities; the United States, Britain, and Japan agreed not to build fortifications on certain of their Pacific territories. And, third, there were some qualitative restraints—limits on the maximum displacement and maximum gun size of specific types of ships; for example, capital ships were not to exceed 35,000 tons nor to carry a gun larger than 16 inches in diameter.

The treaty system for limiting naval armaments remained in effect for about fifteen years. According to most reports the provisions were generally observed fairly rigorously, but assessments of the consequences of the treaty system are more ambiguous.[7] It is true that expen-

6. Aircraft carriers: U.S. and Britain, 135,000 tons each; Japan, 81,000 tons; France and Italy, 60,000 tons each. Heavy cruisers: United States, 180,000 tons; Britain, 146,800 tons; Japan, 108,400 tons. Light cruisers: United States, 143,500 tons; Britain, 192,200 tons; Japan, 100,450 tons. Destroyers: United States and Britain, 150,000 tons each; Japan, 105,500 tons. Submarines: United States, Britain, and Japan, 52,700 tons each. The cruiser limits also specified the number of ships permissible.

7. Some sources report that certain of the signatories did violate the terms of the agreement in the design and construction of warships, although the ships were not actually deployed until after the Washington treaty had expired. For example, the treaty specified a limit of 35,000 tons for battleships (extended to 45,000 by

ditures on and technological developments relating to the types of vessels directly affected by the treaties were slowed perceptibly during this period. It is also true that overall naval expenditures in both the United States and Britain were reduced. But there are alternative explanations for these circumstances.

For one, it has been alleged that even though the main battle fleets remained in the forefront of naval strategy during this period, the performance of submarines during World War I and the promise of carrier-based naval aviation diminished their importance. As a result, some far-sighted naval officials seemed content to let the modernization of the capital ship take a backseat to the development of submarines and aircraft. Some funds were even rechanneled from capital ships into the construction of cruisers and destroyers—an important consideration in the drive to expand the coverage of ship types in the London treaty.

As for overall naval expenditures, assessments of the treaties' consequences in this regard are plagued by the usual problems of determining causality. It can be argued that a backlash of feeling against the military after World War I and broad-based popular discontent with continuing high levels of expenditures on naval forces combined to bring about the talks on limiting naval inventories in the first place. But whether such sentiments could have influenced expenditures on warship construction if the treaties had not been negotiated is debatable. The fact remains that major naval construction programs planned before the 1922 Washington conference did not take place and naval officers, at least, held the conference responsible.

Assessments of the political consequences of the agreements are also indeterminate. There seems to be little evidence to support the once popular contention that the treaties encouraged Japanese expansion in the Pacific while tying the hands of the United States—a possible cause of World War II. On the other hand, there is equally little evidence that the treaties were able, in any tangible sense, to deter the outbreak of new hostilities. More to the point is Hedley Bull's assessment that the naval limitation treaties were merely one aspect of a more basic and far-reaching political understanding among the five powers. This included a temporary distribution of power in the Pacific basin among the United

---

the London treaty) but almost all such vessels laid down during the mid-thirties exceeded this limit when completed in 1938–41. Japan secretly built two 60,000-ton ships in violation of the treaty limits. Clearly, the lack of adequate verification procedures was a problem.

States, Britain, and Japan, and in the Mediterranean between France and Italy; and an Anglo-American understanding with global implications about spheres of commercial and political influence. As part of these broad, largely tacit settlements, the naval treaties ratified existing force ratios, thus formalizing the five-nation decision not to attempt to upset the status quo for the time being.[8] Then in the early and mid-thirties when these fundamental political understandings began to dissolve—at least in the Pacific and the Mediterranean—so did the agreements.

The lessons learned from the Washington and London naval treaties therefore do not augur well for similar treaties in the future. An agreement on limiting naval inventories might bring about economies in military spending for both the United States and the Soviet Union, and it might help to ease international tension, but mutual accommodation and a rough understanding of relative needs and interests will probably have to precede and will not be an automatic consequence of such an agreement.

Alternative Types of Agreement

The three treaties negotiated in the interwar period provide valuable background for any naval arms limitation discussion, but alternatives have to be considered in relation to today's world and superpower dominion. There are many possible arrangements—multilateral as well as bilateral—but this paper focuses on two of the most important. It explores (to the extent possible with data available in the public domain) the advantages and disadvantages of agreements limiting overall naval strengths in the United States and the Soviet Union, and those limiting specific types of ships.

Limits on Overall Capabilities

Differences in the mission priorities of the U.S. and Soviet Navies that lead to sizable differences in the composition and capabilities of their respective forces (see appendix A) make it difficult to devise agreements with ceilings or reductions in specific kinds of forces. A

8. Note that political developments between 1922 and 1930 necessitated adjustments to the prevailing ratios in the London treaty.

promising course to take therefore may be to select a generalized index of overall capability, settle on either a ceiling or a reduction from existing levels based on that index, and permit each side to allocate its resources as it sees fit, so long as they do not exceed the agreed limit. The advantage of this approach is negotiability. It voids most problems connected with equivalencies, trading off Soviet advantage in one area for U.S. advantage in another. By the same token, the benefits of such an agreement are largely symbolic. It would encourage continuing efforts to stabilize U.S.–Soviet relations and resolve existing areas of conflict. It would indicate to third states that the superpowers were aware of the potential dangers of naval competition and that they were willing to initiate measures to avert them. But it is unlikely that it would set the pertinent index low enough to bring about meaningful reductions in present naval force levels. Hence, this sort of arrangement should not be expected to reduce the cost or eliminate the political dangers of the arms race. At best, such an agreement would provide a political climate for further, more significant negotiations. However, if the above approach is considered desirable, what possible indexes of naval capability could be used?

EXPENDITURES. One suggestion is to limit expenditures on naval forces. And this, in fact, has been what the Soviet Union has advocated. It introduced a specific resolution to this end during the 1973 UN General Assembly meeting.[9] Effective control of expenditures could indeed bring about commensurate, if not strictly proportional, limits on naval capabilities over a long period. (Control of operating funds to restrict current spending is probably out of the question.) For example, if limits were set on expenditures for ship construction, for the procurement of naval equipment, and possibly for research and development on naval systems, theoretically, at least, such an arrangement would offer some prospect of reducing naval inventories. The problem would be to devise *effective* limits on expenditures.

Gross disparities between the U.S. and Soviet economies make comparisons of relative expenditures difficult and of limited utility. The

9. Proposal and draft resolution: UN Doc. A/9191, September 25, 1973; revised draft resolution: UN Doc. A/L. 701/Rev. 1., November 26, 1973; final resolution adopted: GA Res. 3093 (XXVIII), December 7, 1973. See also Andrew J. Pierre, "Limiting Soviet and American Conventional Forces," *Survival*, vol. 15 (March/April 1973), pp. 59–64, for a discussion of one U.S.–Soviet effort to reduce expenditures in the mid-sixties.

production of a single unit of output (such as a ship) requires different quantities of inputs (such as manpower, matériel, and capital) from the two economies. And the burden imposed on each society by military consumption of a unit of input, as expressed in opportunity costs, is likely to be quite different in an absolute sense and to vary by type of input. For example, manpower requirements impose a greater financial burden on the United States than the Soviet Union, while the reverse is likely to be the case for capital investments.[10] These problems could be circumvented, in part, by agreeing on a fixed percentage reduction from present expenditure levels (however those expenditures may be expressed), but little can be done about the lack of data.

Although there is often an overwhelming amount of public information regarding the cost of U.S. military forces as a result of the congressional budget process, there is almost none on Soviet military expenditures. The Soviet government furnishes one annual statistic: a figure for total defense outlays. This statistic is generally considered by Western observers to be incomplete and to constitute more of a political signal than an accurate reflection of total expenditures. The Soviet government has never made public data relating to the cost of particular components of its armed forces—such as the Navy—to say nothing of individual expense items—such as the cost of a ship. And while various methodologies have been developed in the West to estimate Soviet military expenditures, the figures arrived at are still suspect. Under such circumstances, verification of an agreement to limit naval expenditures would be difficult if not impossible.[11]

---

10. This is a very complex subject that cannot be covered in a study of this nature. Difficulties in comparing U.S. and Soviet defense expenditures are discussed in greater detail by Robert W. Campbell and others, "Methodological Problems of Comparing the U.S. and the U.S.S.R. Economies," in *Soviet Economic Prospects for the Seventies,* A Compendium of Papers submitted to the Joint Economic Committee, 93 Cong. 1 sess. (1973), pp. 122–46. A new approach to understanding the burden of naval expenditures on the Soviet economy can be seen in Raymond Hutchings, "The Economic Burden of the Soviet Navy," in Michael K. MccGwire (ed.), *Soviet Naval Developments: Capability and Context,* (Praeger, 1973), pp. 210–27.

11. For further discussions of Soviet defense expenditures see: Stanley H. Cohn, "Economic Burden of Defense Expenditures," and Herbert Block, "Value and Burden of Soviet Defense," in *Soviet Economic Prospects for the Seventies,* pp. 147–62 and 175–264, respectively; and International Institute for Strategic Studies, *The Military Balance, 1973/74* (London: International Institute, 1973), pp. 8–9.

MANPOWER. Manpower is a second general index of naval capability that might be useful in arms control agreements. This measure has the same advantage as any generalized index—it voids the problem of evaluating the relative importance of dissimilar types of forces. Compared to controls on expenditures, moreover, manpower limits are more easily verified; particularly if they restrict only manpower assigned to operational forces.

According to the International Institute for Strategic Studies, there are 475,000 people in the Soviet Navy. This figure includes 75,000 in the naval air arm and another 17,000 in the naval infantry. At the end of 1974, the authorized strength of the American Navy was approximately 540,000. To this figure should be added roughly 190,000 people in the Marine Corps and 35,000 in the Coast Guard, since functionally equivalent units are included in the Soviet total. Thus, U.S. naval forces may be as much as 60 percent larger than their Soviet counterparts.[12] If one excludes the U.S. Marines and Coast Guard, and the Soviet naval infantry, the U.S. advantage drops to 20 percent.

These comparisons do not give an accurate picture of relative capabilities, however. For one thing, the two navies are likely to differ in the proportion of men in operational forces—those assigned to ships and aircraft squadrons—and men in various administrative, support, and other categories. For another, they differ in the proportion of total naval manpower that is maintained in deployed (ready-for-combat) forces. Recent U.S. experience has been that about one-third of total manpower is available for use in operating forces, but that only 30 percent of these people (10 percent of total manpower) can be maintained deployed on a continuing basis. The Soviet Navy typically maintains an even smaller share of its manpower deployed. Of course, the share of total manpower in operational forces can be varied over the long term by changing support policies, shifting some jobs to civilians, new basing arrangements, and so forth. It can be varied for shorter periods by rotating crews and postponing normally scheduled maintenance activities.

An agreement specifying a ceiling on the number of people assigned to operational forces would ease the U.S.–Soviet competition in naval armaments and could help to achieve the more general political benefits previously discussed. It would be readily verifiable, because ships and

---

12. This is not really an extreme estimate; one could argue that functions of the Soviet naval air arm are performed in part by the U.S. Air Force and therefore that the U.S. total should be increased further.

aircraft are quite visible to modern intelligence systems, and it is not difficult to derive their normal crew size. Excluding the two navies' support establishments from the limitation would avoid more difficult verification problems. A disproportionate buildup of nonoperational naval personnel would not be too threatening, since the operational forces are the most salient element in both a military and a political sense, and since it would take longer to build or reactivate naval ships than to train their crews, should one nation or the other attempt to circumvent the agreement.

A reasonable first step might be to agree to ceilings of 200,000 and 150,000, respectively, for U.S. and Soviet personnel assigned to operational ships and naval aircraft squadrons. Such a measure would not need more than marginal reductions in existing forces on either side and would permit each state to continue development of its naval capabilities in present directions, so long as new capabilities were made operational at the expense of existing forces. If such an agreement proved to be workable and if its results met the expectations of each side, it might then be possible to reach further agreements that would significantly reduce the two states' naval personnel and, by implication, both their capabilities and costs.

While some disparity between U.S. and Soviet manpower levels is justified because of the present naval balance, setting the precise ratio is a crucial negotiating problem. The United States would sacrifice more than the Soviet Union in moving toward a more equal ceiling. But acknowledging its inferiority would be difficult for the USSR, even though a ceiling on manpower establishing a 4 : 3 ratio of personnel favoring the United States would enable the Soviet Union to retain its present advantage in number of ships.

The only other provisions necessary in this kind of agreement would be those that foreclosed the transfer to other military components of functions presently performed by naval elements. Preferably such an understanding would constitute an integral part of the initial agreement. The inclusion of these provisions might complicate the calculation of manpower ceilings, but it is unlikely that either signatory would be satisfied that its interests were not in jeopardy without them. For example, U.S. surface deployments in some regions are vulnerable to attack by Soviet aircraft carrying air-to-surface missiles; an expansion in the size of this force under the cloak of the Soviet Air Force would be a violation of the intent, if not the letter, of a naval manpower limitation.

Unfortunately, defining provisions limiting the transfer of military functions could be so difficult that the prospects of any agreement on operational manpower limitations would be spoiled.

AGGREGATE TONNAGE. The third type of generalized index of naval capability that should be considered is aggregate tonnage. Tonnage is a better measure of overall capabilities than number of ships, although there is certainly not a one-to-one relationship between tonnage and military effectiveness. A tonnage restriction would be even more easily verified than manpower controls. If it were to reflect the present naval balance, a ceiling on aggregate naval tonnage would strongly favor the United States. There were slightly more than 500 ships in the active U.S. inventory in 1974 that displaced between 5 million and 6 million tons, whereas there were approximately 2,000 ships in the Soviet inventory that were unlikely to displace as much as 3 million tons.

This introduces a fundamental issue that has to be resolved in any naval arms control negotiation: parity. Parity is a desirable objective in any agreement between two great powers, but in certain circumstances one or the other has to insist on a superior position. In negotiating an aggregate tonnage limitation, for example, the United States could argue that its geographic position, its dependence upon transoceanic trade for economic well-being, its commitments and interests overseas, and the status quo in the naval balance are compelling reasons for specifying limits that would give the U.S. Navy quantitative superiority. Soviet acceptance of a markedly inferior position is questionable; they would naturally be sensitive to the political implications of any such arms control arrangement.

The main problem with an aggregate tonnage restriction, just as with any comprehensive agreement based on a generalized measure of naval power, is that it would not foreclose possibly threatening developments in the capabilities of one party or the other. If an agreement permitted each navy to build ships and aircraft of any type and with any characteristics within the overall limit, how effective would it be? Although the situation would probably be more stable than in the absence of any agreement, neither party could be certain that future naval developments would not threaten its interests. Under such an arrangement, for example, the USSR could not be certain that the United States, while adhering strictly to the 6-million-ton limit, would not retire its amphibious warfare forces—primarily useful in supporting U.S. policies in the third world—and construct more ships designed for antisubmarine warfare, which would pose a greater threat to the Soviet Union. Similarly, the United States could not be certain that the Russians would not divert tonnage from mine warfare and coastal defense forces and build more surface warships or attack submarines.

While sizable shifts in the allocation of aggregate tonnage are unlikely, except over a period of decades, and while limiting aggregate tonnage would probably result in shared political benefits, uncertainties of this nature are likely to make both parties reluctant to reach such an agreement. Arrangements limited to particular types of vessels, by contrast, would be less uncertain in their implications for the relative military balance; they are thus likely to be preferred by both sides to comprehensive controls.

Limits on Specific Types of Vessels

Another type of feasible agreement is to limit inventories of particular kinds of vessels. In appendix A is a projection of the size and composition of the U.S. and Soviet Navies in 1980, by ship class. The projection is based on limited data and necessarily incorporates a number of assumptions regarding building rates, retirement ages, and the like. Consequently, it is not likely to be an accurate prediction of the specific number and kinds of ships in the two navies in 1980. However, because of the long lead time involved in the construction of warships (and because of bureaucratic inertia and similar factors), it is difficult to make basic changes in a navy over a relatively short period of time. Thus the actual 1980 force levels are not likely to differ substantially from those forecast. The projection is useful therefore in roughly predicting what the two navies will look like five years from now and how their resources will be distributed among different kinds of forces.

Given reasonably accurate data, there would seem to be a possibility for a U.S.–Soviet agreement to limit the aggregate tonnage and number of ships in three categories of naval forces. Such an agreement would ensure U.S.–Soviet parity in surface warships, give the United States the edge in aircraft carriers, and grant the Soviet Union more attack and cruise-missile submarines. Such an arrangement based on the relative advantages already attained by each superpower and taking into account the two differing conceptions of the utility of naval power could well be the most realistic way of restricting competition in naval armaments.

SURFACE WARSHIPS. Defining the term "warship" precisely is one of the initial difficulties in negotiating any agreement.[13] A rigorous definition would probably include an upper limit on individual ship size and armaments (including the number of helicopters carried) and, of greater significance, would have to define the lower limits of ships in the category. The latter would have to exclude vessels primarily used for coastal defense—such as missile-carrying patrol boats—and would probably have to deal with size, hull configuration, and power plant, as well as armaments.

In 1980, the U.S. Navy is likely to include close to two hundred surface warships displacing, in aggregate, about 1 million tons at full load. The projected Soviet naval force will include about fifteen more warships, displacing about 850,000 tons.[14] Thus the two sides will be near numerical parity in surface warships—a minor Soviet advantage in number of ships being balanced by an 18 percent U.S. advantage in aggregate tonnage. A 200-ship, million-ton ceiling on surface warships suggests itself as an obvious, mutually acceptable limit; lower, but still equal, limits should not be ruled out either.

The resulting two fleets of surface warships, despite their similar overall dimensions, would have differing capabilities. The U.S. force would consist of larger vessels, averaging 5,200 tons displacement at full load compared to 4,200 tons for the Soviet Navy. About half the U.S. force would be concentrated in frigate classes; the Soviet Union would have less than 40 percent of their ships in this grouping, and a greater number of cruisers and destroyers. The United States would be at an advantage in the number of nuclear-powered vessels (ten versus zero for the USSR), and in antisubmarine warfare (ASW) capabilities. While the United States is likely to have more ships equipped with surface-to-air missile (SAM) systems, the Soviets could well have more

13. For the purpose of this discussion, the term "warship" is used in a non-rigorous manner to define a category of surface naval vessels including cruisers, destroyers, and frigates, but excluding vessels whose primary function is to defend coastal waters or to carry aircraft or assault forces.

14. The Soviet figures do not include the two *Moskva*-class helicopter cruisers. Whether or not these ships should be included in the warship category or counted along with aircraft carriers is problematical. Although counted in the latter category here, this is not meant to bias any future considerations. The figures for both sides exclude classes counted in the "other" category in appendix A, such as the Soviet *Nanuchka* and the U.S. *Pegasus*.

Table 2-1. Projection of U.S. and Soviet Aircraft Carriers, by Tonnage Class, 1980

	Number	
Class	United States	USSR
Less than 20,000 tons	7	2
Between 20,000 and 50,000 tons	5	3
More than 50,000 tons	12	0
Total	24	5

Sources: Author's estimates, based on information supplied by Chief of Naval Operations Admiral J. L. Holloway to Representative Les Aspin, July 3, 1974; John E. Moore (ed.), *Jane's Fighting Ships 1973/1974* (Sampson Low, 1973); Robert P. Berman, "Soviet Naval Strength and Deployment," and Michael K. MccGwire, "Current Soviet Warship Construction and Naval Weapons Deployment," in Michael K. MccGwire, Kenneth Boothe, and John McDonnell (eds.), *Soviet Naval Policy: Objectives and Constraints* (Praeger, 1975), pp. 419–23 and 424–51, respectively.

SAM individual fire-control channels available. Other Soviet advantages would be in the number of ships equipped with surface-to-surface missiles, and in such qualitative features as propulsion systems. The two fleets would be nearly the same age, each averaging about nine years.

AIRCRAFT CARRIERS. There is no obvious level at which ceilings on these ships could be established. Moreover, because of the wide range in the size of aircraft carriers, and because the capabilities of these vessels can differ significantly with size, it would probably be desirable to establish sublimits within an overall ceiling. One possible system, based on the distribution of U.S. and Soviet carriers projected for 1980, is shown in Table 2-1.

The projected U.S. force of twenty-four carriers will displace almost 1,300,000 tons in aggregate. Twelve of these vessels are full-size attack carriers, equipped with catapults and arresting gear and capable of handling modern jet aircraft. The balance of the force consists of five *Tarawa*-class assault carriers (about 40,000 tons each) and seven *Iwo Jima*–class assault carriers (about 18,000 tons each). Each of these twelve assault carriers can carry only helicopters or vertical or short takeoff and landing (V/STOL) aircraft, but could be employed in a variety of missions. The projected Soviet force consists of five ships, displacing about 150,000 tons in aggregate. Two are the *Moskva*-class helicopter cruisers, which are used for antisubmarine warfare; the remainder are the new *Kiev*-class carriers whose function is not known as yet. None of the five ships are likely to be equipped with equipment necessary to accommodate horizontal takeoff jet aircraft.

One possible agreement would be to maintain full-size carriers; that is, those with a displacement greater than 50,000 tons or equipped with gear to accommodate horizontal takeoff jet aircraft, as the exclusive preserve of the United States. The United States would be limited to twelve ships in this category; the Soviet Union would not be permitted any. It would probably not be necessary to add a tonnage restriction, since present carriers are probably already as large as these ships are likely to get. The United States is likely to have a less pronounced (two-to-one) advantage both in the number and tonnage of small- and medium-sized carriers. The agreement could specify that this relationship be maintained—say, twelve helicopter and V/STOL carriers for the United States and six for the Soviet Union, displacing in aggregate 330,000 tons and 150,000 tons, respectively.

It is possible that the Soviet Union would find an agreement unacceptable that debarred construction of full-size carriers, even though there are no present indications that the USSR is planning to build this kind of vessel and despite evidence that Soviet evaluations of their military worth is, at best, ambiguous. If so, overall ceilings on aircraft carriers that incorporated a roughly six-to-one advantage to the United States might provide an alternative means of restricting these types of ships.

SUBMARINES. In 1980, the Soviet Union is likely to have more than a 50 percent advantage in the number of nuclear-powered attack submarines. In terms of tonnage, this advantage will be somewhat less, but the difference in the size of the U.S. and Soviet forces will still be significant. Moreover, there is virtually no way that the United States could reduce this gap unilaterally for many years. Also, the USSR is likely to retain 70 to 80 diesel-powered attack submarines in its inventory in 1980, compared to zero in the U.S. inventory. Obviously, any agreement limiting submarines would have to perpetuate some Soviet advantage, particularly in view of the advantage granted to the United States in aircraft carriers.

An agreement limited to nuclear-powered submarines might specify a ceiling of 80 submarines for the United States and 120 for the USSR. If the agreement were extended to diesel-powered vessels, to discourage either side from diverting shipbuilding resources to conventional submarines, the ceilings might be set at 100 for the United States and 200 for the Soviet Union. U.S. and Soviet submarine tonnage limits (including diesel-powered submarines) might be set at 450,000 and 600,000 tons, respectively.

Other factors that might be considered in connection with a submarine limitation is whether there should be a separate sublimit established for submarines equipped with cruise missiles, and whether coastal or other small submarines should be excluded from the limitation. The fact that such provisions would complicate both negotiation and verification of the agreement militates against them.

THE PROPOSED AGREEMENT is summarized in Table 2-2. It is a simple arms control arrangement and hence should be less difficult to negotiate and to verify. By freezing naval forces in these three categories near projected 1980 force levels, the proposal should avoid many potential sources of domestic opposition in both nations. Obviously, it also would be possible to design agreements with proportionally lower limits, but such rollbacks in naval force levels do not appear to be realistic at the present time. The agreement described above would prevent further escalation in U.S.–Soviet naval competition and thus would avoid the economic and political disadvantages of an unrestrained arms race. Additionally, the agreement—despite its largely marginal effect on naval expenditures—should permit the two powers to reap many of the political benefits discussed above. It would symbolize their awareness of the dangers of unrestrained competition in naval armaments and continue the momentum in negotiating other U.S.–Soviet arms agreements. More significant unilateral or negotiated reductions in naval expenditures could then become possible over time.

The agreement would, however, have important drawbacks. It would not place any limitations on land-based naval airpower, small combatants, mine warfare ships, amphibious warfare vessels (except helicopter assault ships), or support and other auxiliary ships. Consequently, it could result in the diversion of additional resources to these areas. Even within the types of ships controlled, the agreement would not include qualitative restraints (except vessel size) and thus could lead to accelerated modernization schedules, the addition of new weapons or electronic systems to existing hulls, and programs to make greater use of nuclear-propulsion systems. Some of these potential difficulties could be avoided if modernization rates were controlled, but this would increase the negotiating problem significantly and would be of doubtful utility. It is also possible that the agreed limits would serve as a floor for future force levels, rather than as a ceiling. In other words, in the face of pressure to reduce spending on naval forces, defense officials could

Table 2-2. Summary of Proposal to Constrain U.S. and Soviet Naval Inventories, by Type of Vessel

Type	Number of ships allowed		Aggregate tonnage allowed	
	United States	USSR	United States	USSR
Warships[a]	200	200	1,000,000	1,000,000
Full-size aircraft carriers[b]	12	0	1,000,000	0
Medium-sized and small aircraft carriers[e]	12	6	330,000	150,000
Attack submarines[d]	100	200	450,000	600,000
Total	324	406	2,780,000	1,750,000

Sources: Same as Table 2-1.
a. Cruisers, destroyers, and frigates.
b. Carriers equipped with catapults and arresting gear or displacing more than 50,000 tons.
c. Carriers less than 50,000 tons; capable of only accommodating helicopters and V/STOL aircraft. Note that a restriction on the length of the flight deck might also be a prudent constraint.
d. Includes diesel-powered submarines and cruise missile equipped submarines.

argue that it was important to maintain forces at the agreed levels, lest a unilateral reduction be interpreted as indicating U.S. willingness to concede superiority to its rival.

The agreement would also present special problems for decision-makers in both the United States and the Soviet Union. In the United States, there might be some concern that the advantage granted to the Soviet Union in attack submarines would have implications for the future strategic balance. Submarine-based antisubmarine warfare is at present the most likely potential threat to sea-based strategic systems. There might thus be concern that the advantage granted to the USSR in the number of attack submarines could result in a significantly greater Soviet strategic capability. There might also be concern that the compensatory advantage granted to the United States in aircraft carriers would become less important. This would be based on two assumptions: first, aircraft carriers are vulnerable to cruise missiles launched from submarines, surface ships, and the air; and second, in the future, the United States would have less propensity to intervene with air power or ground forces overseas and hence would have less need for aircraft and helicopter carriers. Finally, U.S. decisionmakers might be concerned about possible "offensive" uses of the Soviet Union's large number of smaller combatants—a type of ship that would not be controlled by the agreement.

In the Soviet Union, officials would be gratified at the agreement's implication that the USSR had attained equal status with the United States as a naval power. Concern would focus, however, on those provisions that would perpetuate the Soviet Union's inferior position regarding sea-based air power. Despite concern as to the vulnerability of aircraft carriers, some naval officers argue that without sizable air forces based at sea a navy's flexibility is severely limited. The recent appearance of the Soviet Union's first medium-sized aircraft carrier would seem to indicate that this school of thought is not absent in the USSR. A secondary concern to Soviet decisionmakers might be whether the advantage granted to the USSR in number of attack submarines would be sufficient to compensate for the marked qualitative advantages held by the United States in submarine technology.

CHAPTER THREE

LIMITATIONS ON NAVAL DEPLOYMENTS

In recent years, what little attention has been paid to naval arms control has been concerned, almost exclusively, with measures of deployment limitation. The Soviet Union broached the issue several times although there is reason (discussed later in the chapter) to discount the seriousness of its proposals. The U.S. Senate has also shown interest particularly in limiting deployments to the Indian Ocean.

Previous International Agreements[1]

This approach to arms limitation has been tried before. In two areas—the Great Lakes and the Black Sea—agreements have lasted some years and been reasonably successful. These and two other agreements are reviewed below to determine what underlying conditions have led to their relative success or failure.

Rush-Bagot Agreement of 1817

The longest-lasting and most successful of the international agreements that constrained naval deployments in the past is the Rush-Bagot agreement of 1817.[2] This treaty limited U.S. and British (later Canadian) naval deployments and vessel construction on the Great Lakes. The agreement restricted each side to four vessels, each not to exceed 100 tons nor to carry a cannon larger than 18 pounds. Two ships were

1. This section was prepared with the assistance of Louisa Thoron.
2. Exchange of Notes Relative to Naval Forces on the American Lakes. See Hunter Miller (ed.), *Treaties and Other International Acts of the United States of America* (Washington, D.C.: Government Printing Office), vol. 2, Document 38, pp. 645–47.

deployed on the upper lakes, one on Lake Ontario, and one on Lake Champlain. The agreement (revised in 1922 and 1939 to exempt revenue and police cutters, and training ships, and to permit construction as long as the new ships did not remain on the Lakes) has remained in force ever since.

The Rush-Bagot agreement came about, at American instigation, after Britain had expressed concern about the situation on the Lakes during negotiations to settle the War of 1812. Since then there have been only two serious diplomatic exchanges regarding possible treaty violations: in 1838, when Britain increased its forces on the Lakes ostensibly to counter activities of the Canadian Patriots, an independence movement; and during the U.S. Civil War when the United States increased its forces to stem the activities of Confederate raiders based in Canada. Otherwise there have been virtually no disputes. Given the obsolescence of the specific restrictions contained in the agreement, this success should be attributed to the good relations established between the United States and Canada, rather than to the agreement itself.

Montreux Convention of 1936

Another agreement that has withstood greater political stress fairly successfully has been the Montreux convention, which regulates passage through the Turkish Straits and naval deployments in the Black Sea.[3] The Montreux convention, signed in 1936, was the last of a series of arrangements governing the movement of merchant and naval vessels in these waters: the Treaty of Paris (1856), the Treaty of London (1871), the Treaty of Sèvres (1920), and the Lausanne Convention (1923), all contained provisions regulating the deployment of warships and other vessels in the Black Sea and the Straits.

Article 18 of the Montreux convention governs the deployment of

3. Convention Regarding the Regime of the Straits with Protocol Signed at Montreux. For a fuller discussion of the agreement and its international implications, see Harry N. Howard, "The Turkish Straits after the Montreux Convention," *Foreign Affairs*, vol. 15 (October 1936), pp. 199–202; Cyril E. Black, "The Turkish Straits and the Great Powers," *Foreign Policy Reports*, vol. 23, no. 14 (1947), pp. 174–82; Harry N. Howard, "The Turkish Straits after World War II: Problems and Prospects," *Balkan Studies*, vol. 11, no. 1 (1970), pp. 35–60; and Ferenc Vali, *The Turkish Straits and NATO* (Stanford: Hoover Institute, 1972). The text of the agreement is given in Ralph H. Magnus (ed.), *Documents on the Middle East* (Washington, D.C.: American Enterprise Institute, 1969).

warships in the Black Sea by nonlittoral powers. There are four provisions:

• The aggregate tonnage of such ships is not to exceed 30,000 tons (this was later increased to 45,000 tons).

• No single nonlittoral state can deploy ships whose gross tonnage is more than two-thirds of this figure.

• An exception can be made, if authorized by the Turkish government on humanitarian grounds, for a ship or ships whose gross tonnage does not exceed 8,000 tons.

• No warship belonging to a nonlittoral state can remain in the Black Sea for more than twenty-one days.

These provisions still effectively constrain the ability of nonlittoral states to maintain a standing naval force in the Black Sea, except for limited periods of time.

The Montreux convention is a remarkable document in a number of respects, not least of which is its longevity. Despite blatant disregard of the agreement during World War II, and even though the convention technically expired in 1956, the signatories continue to modify their behavior so as to adhere to the letter, if not fully the spirit, of the agreement. This has occurred in spite of drastic changes in naval technology since 1936 and, more important, a radically altered international situation. Unlike the Rush-Bagot agreement, which seems to owe its continued effectiveness mainly to the absence of serious conflict between its signatories, the Montreux convention has come under heavy fire from different sources on a number of occasions. Between the end of World War II and 1953, the Soviet Union made several serious efforts to bring about major revisions in the treaty; there have been less sustained campaigns since that time. Apparently, however, its provisions are sufficiently flexible for the signatories still to find it in their interest to comply, at least to a minimal extent, with its requirements.

Other Historical Examples

Two other agreements concluded during the interwar years also deserve mention.

In 1931, Turkey and the Soviet Union concluded a naval limitation agreement. This agreement, in the form of a protocol to a broader Treaty of Friendship, specified a form of deployment limitation. The two parties agreed not to acquire new warships "intended to strengthen the fleet in the Black Sea or neighboring seas."[4] The agreement was not very effective. Despite its renewal in 1936, and the fact that it remained formally in effect until the outbreak of the Second World War, the Soviet Black Sea Fleet was increased significantly during this period.

Finally, there is the Nyon agreement of 1937—an arrangement that restricted the deployment of submarines in the Mediterranean.[5] The agreement, initiated by Britain and France, stemmed from the sinking of merchant ships by Italian (although officially "unidentified") submarines in 1936 and 1937 during the civil war in Spain. The Nyon agreement barred submarines from the Mediterranean, except in specified areas for naval exercises, or if transit was announced beforehand and they were accompanied by a surface ship. Moreover, the agreement gave Britain and France the right to patrol the region (with certain exceptions) in order to enforce these regulations, and included the right to attack any submarines found submerged in a prohibited zone. The Nyon agreement was signed by Bulgaria, Egypt, France, Great Britain, Greece, Rumania, the Soviet Union, Turkey, and Yugoslavia. Later on, a supplementary arrangement was reached with Italy, which was also given enforcement responsibilities in particular zones within the region. The agreement apparently was relatively ineffective and was terminated at the outbreak of World War II. It is reported that Britain and France, despite frequent contacts with submarines in violation of the agreement, as a matter of policy never exercised their enforcement responsibilities.

Success or Failure?

Have these historical examples any lessons for future agreements to limit naval deployments? They are important for two reasons.

First, these agreements establish several precedents. Despite their

4. Quoted in Richard Dean Burns and Seymour L. Chapin, "Near Eastern Naval Limitation Pacts, 1930–1931," *East European Quarterly*, vol. 4, no. 1 (1970), pp. 72–87.

5. International Agreement for Collective Measures against Piratical Attacks in the Mediterranean by Submarines, signed September 14, 1937, at Nyon, France. The Nyon agreement is discussed in Arnold J. Toynbee, *Survey of International Affairs: 1937* (Oxford University Press, 1938), pp. 322–23, 345, 385. Based on discussions with British naval officers who had been in the Mediterranean at the time, however, Toynbee's review is rather optimistic.

frequent allusion to the indivisibility of freedom of the oceans, it is apparent that great powers have found it in their interest, at times, to agree to limitations on their right to deploy warships on the high seas. The agreements demonstrate various ways in which these restrictions could be accomplished, ranging from simple pledges of good intention to arrangements for specific ceilings on permissible tonnage and duration of naval deployment or complete exclusion. In one agreement some of the signatories were actually given authority to enforce these controls.

Second, the agreements have one significant point in common with the Washington and London treaties limiting naval inventories—the success or failure of naval arms control measures cannot be isolated from the broader political issues involving the signatories. If relations among the parties to an agreement take a turn for the worse, the agreed limits on naval activity—no matter how well the provisions are designed—are unlikely to be observed. Similarly, so long as there are good relations among signatories—such as those between the United States and Canada—an arms control arrangement can survive long beyond the time when its provisions are pertinent to the contemporary armaments situation. This is not to say that the specific content of an agreement is unimportant. Obviously, agreements can be better or worse in terms of the clarity and restrictiveness of their provisions, the degree to which their limits can be verified, their implications for short- and long-term stability in terms of military balance, and the like. It is to say, however, that any arrangement to restrict naval arms is only likely to be successful within a broader political context and when relations are not openly hostile. Arms control agreements can mitigate specific problems and short-term war risks, but over the longer term they can, by themselves, make only a limited contribution to the maintenance of amicable relations among states.

Alternative Types of Agreements

Any proposal to limit naval deployments implies a complicated and sometimes perplexing set of tradeoffs between potential risks and benefits. Two kinds of agreements are discussed in this paper: denuclearization and disengagement in regions of potential conflict. The latter is discussed in relation to the Indian Ocean and the Mediterranean Sea.

Denuclearization

Just as in the case of inventory limitations, agreements to limit naval deployments can be either broad or narrow in terms of the range of military systems that are restricted. The most narrow forms of agreement prohibit certain kinds of weapons on board ships in particular regions. This type of agreement is discussed most frequently in relation to measures that would bar nuclear weapons from certain seas or oceans, an approach to arms control known as denuclearization. At the 1974 summit meeting, for example, General Secretary Brezhnev is reported to have proposed to President Nixon that the two superpowers agree to ban all nuclear-armed warships from the Mediterranean.[6]

The broad appeal of this type of arms control device stems from two rather simple notions: first, that any limitation on nuclear weaponry is a step in the right direction; and second, that denuclearization is a mechanism whereby the risks of superpower naval confrontation can be reduced. A closer look at the problem, however, leads to considerable skepticism.

Aside from strategic ballistic missiles, the United States keeps nuclear munitions on some of its warships for three kinds of weapon systems: nuclear ordnance for tactical aircraft based on aircraft carriers, nuclear warheads for surface-to-air missiles, and nuclear explosives for some kinds of antisubmarine weapons. The USSR, which has no tactical aircraft based at sea, presumably does have the latter two kinds of weapons. In addition, the Soviet Union can put nuclear warheads on some of its sea-based, surface-to-surface cruise missiles. Nuclear munitions, however, frequently may not be deployed on Soviet warships, due to the general Soviet tendency to maintain rigid controls on nuclear weaponry. Obviously, command and control problems are multiplied when a nuclear weapon is deployed on a warship far from the Soviet command structure. Keeping nuclear warheads on warships is also practically inconvenient because of the relatively small size of Soviet naval vessels. One of the things the USSR sacrifices because it builds smaller ships, and thereby incurs lower costs, is reload capacity and automated magazines and reload systems. Thus Soviet planners must choose carefully in loading ordnance on their ships; it is believed that they tend to select

6. *New York Times,* July 22, 1974. Radio Moscow; reported in Foreign Broadcast Information Service (FBIS), *Daily Report: Soviet Union,* July 24, 1974.

conventional munitions most frequently because it is the form of weaponry most likely to be employed under normal circumstances.

It should be noted at the outset that the utility of some sea-based nuclear weapons, even in a tactical military sense, is questionable. It is not evident, for example, that a frigate would have a better chance of sinking an enemy submarine using nuclear rather than conventional explosives.[7] Besides, even on U.S. warships, nuclear ordnance must compete with conventional munitions for scarce magazine space. These difficulties—combined with the low-probability estimate of nuclear weapons ever being used for tactical purposes—make a plausible military argument for abandoning certain types.

It would be very difficult to verify an agreement that permitted some kinds of nuclear weapons to remain on warships but prohibited others. Verification of even a total ban on nuclear weapons at sea is difficult, because the detection of radioactive material is not possible except at short distances, but mutually acceptable arrangements could possibly be devised. Such arrangements would have to include the exchange of visits by inspection teams, although the extent of their probings could probably be restricted. A partial ban, on the other hand, requires a very elaborate and intrusive inspection system which neither side would probably find acceptable. Submarines are, moreover, likely to be excluded from any denuclearization agreement.

Additionally, it is not apparent that there would be much to gain from an agreement that banned nuclear weapons in specific ocean areas. Such an agreement would imply only modest savings, if any, in military spending. It would not appreciably affect the political and psychological consequences of naval confrontations. Nor would it directly reduce the broader risks associated with competition in naval armaments. An agreement *would* please those third nations that have carried on diplomatic campaigns to bar nuclear weapons in particular geographic regions, such as the Indian Ocean. It would also reduce the risk of accidental or unauthorized release of nuclear weapons.

Finally it can be argued that, with a denuclearization agreement, the

7. Nuclear munitions increase the lethal radius of the explosive, but this sometimes may be more than offset by the lower performance of sensors—such as radars and sonars—and command and control systems caused by electromagnetic radiations and other side effects of nuclear explosions. Moreover, technological developments, such as wire-guided torpedoes, which have greatly increased the accuracy of conventional weapons, reduce the incentive to use nuclear weapons.

demarcation line between conventional and nuclear war would be more distinct. Tactical nuclear weapons provide a bridge between conventional and strategic nuclear war and thereby make the transition from one to the other somewhat easier. The damage they cause is not much more serious than that caused by conventional munitions. Consequently, it is possible that the superpowers could be led, small step by small step, from a strictly conventional war to a strategic nuclear conflict. Prohibiting these smaller nuclear weapons would possibly make the dividing line between the two types of conflict more distinct and less likely to be breached.

On the other hand, it can also be argued that the risk of a gradual escalation to strategic nuclear war from conventional conflict is a far more serious problem for ground forces than for the Navies of the United States and the Soviet Union. In fact, if there had to be a tactical nuclear war between the superpowers, it would be better to fight it at sea—where the collateral damage to civilian facilities would be minimal and where the combatant forces could be better controlled and more easily disengaged—than on land. Consequently, this argument concludes, it makes little sense to bar nuclear ordnance for sea-based weapons while their land-based equivalents remain uncontrolled.

Thus there does not seem to be any compelling argument that limitations on nuclear weapons at sea provide more than ambiguous military, economic, or political benefits. Moreover, attainment of such an agreement would require the United States to make a far greater sacrifice than the USSR. U.S. aircraft carriers retain a residual role in U.S. strategic planning. Removing nuclear weapons when they are to be deployed in the Mediterranean would curtail their effectiveness in this role. Aircraft carriers also have a key part in U.S. planning for NATO contingencies. Under the strategy of "flexible response," the capability to fight a tactical nuclear war in Europe is an important element of the U.S. military posture. Removing nuclear weapons from carriers in the Mediterranean would decrease this capability, and would thus be viewed with alarm by some U.S. allies. Finally, aside from the sparing use of nuclear weapons on Soviet naval vessels, their role in Soviet military strategy is only derivative. They would be used, for example, not to affect the outcome of a land battle in Europe directly, but to counter a possible U.S. attempt to project nuclear power into the primary combat arena from the sea.

Given the uneven sacrifice called for by a Mediterranean denuclearization accord, an imbalance of which Soviet planners must be fully aware, and the verification problem previously mentioned (a difficulty usually of greater concern to the United States in arms control negotiations), the motives behind Brezhnev's 1974 proposal appear suspect.

Naval Disengagement in Regions of Potential Conflict

The most important aim of naval arms control is to reduce the risk of military conflict stemming from sporadic confrontations between the U.S. and Soviet Navies in regions where, and at times when, international tension runs high. The most direct way to meet this goal would be to restrict the size and duration of warship deployments to regions where such confrontation is likely to occur. Obviously, a zero limit would ensure that no naval confrontation occurs; but such a goal is now unrealistic. It may be possible to negotiate limits above zero, however, whose practical consequences would approximate the advantages of complete disengagement.

In fact, on several occasions the Soviet Union has indicated an interest in negotiating such limitations with the United States. There is clear evidence of disagreement within the USSR as to the advisability of such measures, however, and its interest slackened perceptibly during 1974.

The USSR has called for naval disengagement in various ocean areas on numerous occasions since the early 1950s. These proposals tended to focus on the Mediterranean Sea, the Indian Ocean (or specific subregions of these basins); a few related to the Pacific Ocean and the Baltic Sea. The early initiatives can be dismissed without comment.[8] Having token or no forces of its own in the regions mentioned, the Soviet Union's early proposals can be interpreted as straightforward bids for the United States to remove its military forces in exchange for various intangible benefits—maybe "tranquility" and "good-will." Although the Soviets probably did not expect the United States to take them

8. Examples of these proposals may be seen in the following: "Note from the Soviet Foreign Ministry to the American Embassy Transmitting a Draft Declaration on Nonintervention in the Middle East" (February 1, 1957), in U.S. Department of State, *Documents on Disarmament, 1957–59*, pp. 742–46; "Soviet Note to the United States on Nuclear-Free Zone in Mediterranean" (May 20, 1963), *Documents on Disarmament, 1963*, pp. 187–93; "Statement by Soviet Representative (Roshchin) to the Eighteen Nation Disarmament Committee" (August 13, 1968), *Documents on Disarmament, 1968*, pp. 572–79.

seriously, they may have believed that the proposals would create inhospitable local conditions for the Western military presence and, coincidentally, help to align the USSR more closely with the aspirations of the third world.

More recent proposals compel greater attention, however, if only because the Soviet buildup of naval and other military forces in the Mediterranean and Indian Ocean regions gives greater weight to their bargaining power. In June 1971, General Secretary Brezhnev called for negotiations with the United States on the mutual limitation of naval deployments:

We have never considered, and do not now consider, that it is an ideal situation when the navies of the great powers are cruising about for long periods far from their own shores, and we are prepared to solve this problem, but to solve it, as they say, on an equal basis. On the basis of such principles, the Soviet Union is ready to discuss any proposals.[9]

He mentioned the Mediterranean Sea and the Indian Ocean specifically as regions of interest. This public pronouncement followed private soundings by Soviet diplomats earlier in the year, thus indicating the seriousness of the proposal.[10]

Brezhnev's initiative led to some contacts between U.S. and Soviet diplomats but not, apparently, to substantive discussions.[11] The proposal was reaffirmed frequently in the Soviet press and on the radio for about two years.[12] Almost all restatements, however, appeared in articles

9. Speech by General Secretary Leonid I. Brezhnev of the Central Committee, Communist Party of the Soviet Union; reported in FBIS, *Daily Report: Soviet Union*, June 14, 1971.

10. See testimony by former Under Secretary of State U. Alexis Johnson in *Executive Agreements with Portugal and Bahrain*, Hearings before the Senate Committee on Foreign Relations, 92 Cong. 2 sess. (1972), p. 20; and also testimony by Deputy Director J. Owen Zurhellen, U.S. Arms Control and Disarmament Agency, in *Proposed Expansion of U.S. Military Facilities in the Indian Ocean*, Hearings before the House Committee on Foreign Affairs, 93 Cong. 2 sess. (1972), pp. 6–7.

11. See Johnson and Zurhellen testimony in ibid., and report in *Washington Post*, February 2, 1972. For brief accounts of the National Security Council deliberations on Indian Ocean naval limitations, see *Melbourne Age,* April 27, 1971, and *Sydney Morning-Herald*, April 28, 1971.

12. See, for example, "The New Soviet Initiatives: The Ball Is Now in Washington's Court," *SSHA: Ekonomika, Politika, Ideologiya*, No. 8 (July 12, 1971); reported in FBIS, *Daily Report: Soviet Union*, August 24, 1971. Radio Moscow, "The Mediterranean Must Become a Sea of Peace and Calm," Peace and Progress Series (a series of broadcasts in French and English aimed at an African audience), January 20, 1972, in French, and October 19, 1972, in English; reported in FBIS, ibid., January 21, 1972, and October 27, 1972, respectively.

by individuals attached to various Soviet social science academies—such as the Academy for the Study of the U.S.A.—or in radio broadcasts, neither source being likely to inspire confidence in the degree to which the proposals were held seriously by Soviet defense officials.

Evidence of disagreement within the USSR is illustrated in the contrasting views publicized by Soviet military representatives. In late 1972, Admiral S. N. Gorshkov, commander-in-chief of the Soviet Navy, launched a spirited attack on measures of naval arms control in an article published in the Soviet *Naval Digest*.[13] Six months later, Brezhnev's proposal was reported on favorably by Colonel General N. V. Ogarkov, first deputy chief of the Armed Forces General Staff, in an interview published in *Red Star*—the major journal of the Soviet armed forces.[14] The inclusion of General Ogarkov's statement regarding mutual naval disengagement was clearly no accident and was probably meant to indicate that Admiral Gorshkov's views were not shared by the Defense Ministry or, at least, that the military leadership was prepared to accede to Secretary Brezhnev's desire to maintain this possible opening for negotiations with the United States.

Soviet interest now seems to have waned. In January 1974, when the U.S. Navy announced its plan to expand support facilities on Diego Garcia, a massive propaganda campaign was launched in the Soviet media. At no point does it seem that the Brezhnev proposal was mentioned during the campaign. This is strange, as the proposal would seem to provide a natural contrast to announced U.S. plans for Soviet propagandists. The 1974 Brezhnev summit proposal for Mediterranean denuclearization, compared to disengagement, would seem to be a retreat from serious interest in naval arms control because the unequal nature of U.S. and Soviet tradeoffs in a denuclearization agreement would rule out serious consideration of such measures by the United States. Admiral Gorshkov's prompt endorsement of Mediterranean denuclearization, contrasted to his failure to back the 1971 naval disengagement proposal, underscores the view that the 1974 summit proposal represents declining Soviet interest in naval arms control rather than a serious new initiative.[15]

13. S. N. Gorshkov, "Navies in Peace and War," in *Morskoi Sbornik* (*Naval Digest*), Nos. 9 & 10, 1972.

14. *Krasnaya Zvezda* (*Red Star*), July 10, 1973, p. 3; reported in FBIS, *Daily Report: Soviet Union,* July 13, 1973. Ogarkov had been the Soviet military's representative on the SALT delegation.

15. Gorshkov's endorsement was given in an interview broadcast over Radio Moscow; reported in FBIS, ibid., August 2, 1974. A study of Soviet interest in

A Proposed Disengagement Agreement

If a persuasive case can be made that naval disengagement in a particular region would serve U.S. interests, the Soviet Union's declining interest is not sufficient reason for the United States to rule it out. Some in the USSR evidently still see at least tactical advantage in naval arms control, and a U.S. approach could reinforce their position. The primary issue for U.S. decisionmakers is whether some form of naval disengagement would benefit the United States; not whether the political climate is right for negotiation.

An evaluation of the U.S. interest, in turn, depends to some degree on the specific content of the proposal. To provide a tangible basis for discussing the benefits and risks of a naval disengagement agreement and to illustrate the mechanisms necessary to control naval deployments, I have drafted such an arms control regime. It is included as appendix B, applied to the Indian Ocean.[16]

The main features of the proposed agreement are summarized in this chapter. Subsequent chapters examine the merits of the proposal in relation to naval disengagement in the Mediterranean and the Indian Ocean.

THE PROPOSAL IN BRIEF. The agreement prohibits standing naval deployments, that is, the maintenance of a permanent naval presence, in the designated region. Deployments for short periods for specific purposes, such as ceremonial visits or emergencies, are permitted; but these are also controlled by limiting the overall number of vessels or tonnage of vessels that each signatory is permitted to deploy to the region at any one time, and by limiting the time that individual vessels are allowed to remain in the area. This restriction, which follows the precedent of Article 18 of the Montreux convention (governing naval deployments by nonlittoral states to the Black Sea), is an effective way of making operational the prohibition against standing deployments and constitutes a more realistic negotiating goal than a flat prohibition against any naval deployments by the superpowers. If the limits are defined at a low

---

naval arms control may be found in a paper by Anne M. Kelly and Charles Petersen, "Recent Changes in Soviet Naval Policy: The Prospects for Arms Limitation in the Mediterranean and Indian Ocean" (Arlington, Va.: Center for Naval Analyses, 1975; forthcoming).

16. The draft is designed simply to illustrate the type of agreement being discussed. While the substantive ideas are important, the provisions and the actual levels mentioned at which various limitations are defined are not material.

enough level—particularly the maximum time that individual vessels are allowed to remain in the area—the effect would be nearly the same as a flat prohibition.

Essentially, these provisions reduce the risk of preemptive attack associated with the tactical military situation that develops when the two superpower fleets are deployed in a relatively confined area. Once such an agreement is concluded, it is less likely that the two fleets will serve as visible symbols of national commitment in the third world and, hence, as the leading edge of superpower involvement in local conflicts. At the same time, allowing intermittent deployments serves several military and political functions and, in so doing, it also reduces opposition to the agreements in both the United States and the USSR.

Intermittent deployments are permitted for two types of purposes:

Normal deployments. Warships of the signatories are permitted to enter the designated region for brief periods of time in order to carry out normal peacetime naval activities—for example, to traverse the region, to make port visits on ceremonial occasions, and to conduct periodic familiarization cruises. These activities serve mainly to increase superpower confidence that their respective naval forces are sufficiently familiar with the region so that, should the agreement break down, they would be able to reenter and deal with any contingency in an effective and timely manner. Normal deployments are to be reported in advance to a joint control commission, explained below, and are limited in size and frequency as mentioned above.

Emergency deployments. The signatories are also permitted to deploy warships to the region in order to protect the lives of their nationals in emergencies. These deployments need only be reported a brief time, say twenty-four hours, in advance. The other signatory is given the privilege of matching any emergency deployment, should it choose to do so.

This second provision is probably the Achilles' heel of the agreement in that it provides a means for either signatory to violate the spirit, if not the letter, of the treaty. The deployment of naval forces, ostensibly to protect the lives of nationals, also could provide a cloak for warships used to support national political objectives. Such a provision is likely to be mandatory, however, if the superpowers are to subscribe to an agreement of this nature. In its operational effect, the provision is the equivalent of the phrase included in most arms control agreements that permits the signatories to withdraw should they perceive that their "supreme national interests had been jeopardized." In each case, the inclusion of a legal escape route from negotiated restraints, based on subjective interpretations of events, permits continued adherence to the dicta of international law in the face of potentially calamitous developments that would otherwise lead to their violation. One can imagine, for example, a situation developing in which the lives of large numbers of American citizens residing in a foreign nation are threatened, in which diplomatic processes have failed, and in which, therefore, the President feels compelled to attempt an armed evacuation. Without inclusion of the emergency provision, under such conditions the President may well proceed with the evacuation even though it violates the terms of the disengagement agreement. Such a step, aside from its immediate dangers, can have long-lasting repercussions for other arms control agreements and for general relations with the USSR; and it can also diminish the confidence of other nations in the viability of agreements that they themselves are already planning to negotiate with the United States.

Some would argue that inclusion of the emergency provision constitutes an open invitation to violation of the agreement and thus might cause greater damage than benefit. In my view, the above rationale argues against such an interpretation, and there are also two additional safeguards. First, the fact that the nation wishing to deploy ships in an area would officially have to invoke an emergency—a measure that by itself is likely to raise international tension—should discourage such a step in marginal situations. Second, the prospect of another signatory matching any emergency deployment should undercut much of the advantage that a state might foresee from its own initial deployment and therefore deter frivolous use of the provision.

CRITICAL NEGOTIATION ISSUES. Negotiations on this form of disengagement will have to focus on how to limit deployments and the types of ships restricted; these will determine what each side has to gain.

The level and form of control for intermittent deployments is the important issue. Given the gross differences in the structure and composition of the two superpower navies, whether to use number of hulls or tonnage of ships as the operational measure of control is more than an academic question.[17] As U.S. ships tend to be much larger than their

17. Each of these measures, of course, is only a proxy for actual naval capability. Ideally, more refined indexes should be used but disagreement on what are the best measures and the complex negotiating required rule out greater refinements.

Soviet counterparts, an agreement based on equal tonnage restrictions would permit the USSR to deploy a larger number of vessels. If both states were bound by equal restrictions on the number of hulls, the United States would be able to deploy a greater amount of tonnage and presumably a greater capability.[18] Clearly it is necessary to negotiate a combination of controls, and a combination that permits certain asymmetries to account for basic differences in the two navies.

The other critical question relates to the types of ships included. One approach would be to apply controls only to "warships and submarines," or "combatant vessels"—excluding support ships. This has two advantages and one disadvantage. It would permit each side to station unarmed vessels in the designated region to monitor compliance with the agreement, thereby increasing its likely durability. It would also alleviate definitional problems. The Soviet Union and, to a lesser extent, the United States use civilian vessels (for example, oil tankers and supply ships) for certain military or paramilitary functions. On the other hand, excluding noncombatant naval vessels would make verification of the agreement more difficult and possibly invite various forms of noncompliance.

Another approach would be to limit deployment of *all* naval vessels, not just warships; but in this case it would be difficult to discriminate among auxiliary vessels. A third approach might be to set variable limitations for different classes of vessels; but an agreement with this provision would be even more difficult.

The agreement described in appendix B also prohibits the signatories from maintaining shore installations for the support of naval vessels— communications stations, ordnance and fuel depots, repair yards, dry docks, and the like. Use of facilities that are under the sovereignty of another nation is also prohibited. (The latter is an important means by which the Soviet Union now provides support to its ships.) These pro-

18. For example, the newest type of U.S. destroyer—of the *Spruance* class— displaces more than 7,000 tons, while new Soviet destroyers—of the *Krivak* class —displace 4,800 tons. Modern U.S. aircraft carriers displace around 90,000 tons, while the first Soviet carriers displace no more than 40,000. Thus an agreement to limit both fleets to no more than five ships in the region at any one time—say a carrier and four destroyers—would leave the United States with a two-to-one advantage in tonnage (118,000 tons compared with 59,200 tons for the Soviet Union). An agreement to limit both fleets to 90,000 tons deployed, on the other hand, would permit the USSR to send in a carrier and ten destroyers, while the United States could dispatch only a carrier without any escorts: an untenable situation for U.S. naval planners. (See John E. Moore (ed.), *Jane's Fighting Ships 1973/1974* [Sampson Low, 1973].)

hibitions reduce the risk of a sudden violation and the introduction of major naval forces without notice into the region, since the absence of such facilities would make it difficult to maintain large standing deployments for protracted periods of time.

Difficulties arise in discriminating between shore facilities supporting naval deployments and other military installations, and in the precise definition of those areas in which naval support bases are to be prohibited. If each party is required to draw up a list of those installations it proposes to include *and those it proposes not to include,* and then to negotiate on the basis of these lists, the first problem might be alleviated; but the second is likely to be more troublesome. For example, some U.S. naval facilities are located in nations such as Thailand and Australia, bordering on the Indian Ocean, that provide support to U.S. naval forces in both the Indian Ocean and the Pacific; their disposition is therefore ambiguous.

IMPLEMENTATION AND VERIFICATION. Finally, any agreement of this type should include a full set of safeguards to ensure that each nation's interests are protected and that confidence in the treaty is maintained. These provisions would include periodic renegotiation and amendment; the allowance of unilateral withdrawal (following a delay), if one signatory perceived that its "supreme national interests" had been jeopardized; and arrangements for monitoring compliance.

Each signatory is expected to depend primarily on unilateral national means for verification. Nonetheless, it would be useful (as I have suggested in appendix B) to establish a joint control commission charged with overseeing implementation of the agreement and its continued smooth operation. The functions of the commission, consisting of representatives of each signatory and of the states in the region, is to report on activities and to serve as a forum for continued consultation and negotiation. Nations deploying forces to the region would inform the commission in advance, which would then monitor and report their compliance with or deviation from prescribed limitations. Involving local states in verification of the agreement is an additional insurance against cheating or other forms of noncooperation. Under a commission so constituted, a violation would be not only against the other signatory but also against the states of the region. Verification problems specific to each potential region are discussed later in the paper.

CHAPTER FOUR

DISENGAGEMENT IN THE MEDITERRANEAN

The potential gains from naval disengagement are greatest in the Mediterranean. Its strategic location and the many local rivalries make it a critical area for U.S.–Soviet military relations. As the two superpowers have come to commit themselves, in varying degree, to the defense of states in the region, local conflicts have tended to become polarized along East-West lines. Both the United States and the Soviet Union now deploy large and powerful fleets in the region; and both view developments there as important, if not vital, to their national security.

The U.S. military presence in the Mediterranean stems from three major concerns. Initial postwar U.S. deployments (1947–48) were prompted by the USSR's support of insurgents in the Greek civil war and by Soviet demands for military bases and other concessions in Turkey. Suspicions as to Soviet designs on Greece and Turkey, and by implication on other areas in southern Europe, is one important justification for the U.S. military presence in the Mediterranean. Soviet military and political involvement with the Arab world since 1955, and the growth of Soviet naval forces in the Mediterranean since 1964, have aggravated this anxiety about the security of NATO's "southern flank." How much American fears have been alleviated by the expulsion of Soviet combat units from Egypt in July 1972, the altered character of U.S.–Egyptian relations, and the effect of the 1974 Cyprus crisis on U.S. relations with Greece and Turkey remains to be seen. In the meantime, however, an important purpose of the U.S. military presence in the Mediterranean is related to the NATO commitment: to deter Soviet aggression against Greece and Turkey, to combat any military offensive in the region should deterrence fail, and to carry out various combat missions against the Soviet Union and its allies should war break out on NATO's central front.

Second, U.S. military forces serve purposes in the Mediterranean and elsewhere in the Middle East besides those connected with NATO. A powerful U.S. military presence is considered useful in deterring aggression. It reassures Israel as to the U.S. commitment and dissuades potential adversaries because of the implicit threat of U.S. involvement. In times of crisis U.S. forces can signal intent, make threats, and generally exert a stabilizing influence over the course of events. They are also believed to help maintain U.S. influence in other local nations, such as Jordan, which are not allied to the United States. The proximity of sizable U.S. forces tends to help maintain the authority of Western-oriented regimes.

Third, for reasons of geography and the technical limitations of certain military systems, some military installations in the Mediterranean region are important to the United States in terms of the overall strategic balance. There are radar sites in Turkey, a submarine base at Rota, Spain, and installations in other nations along the Mediterranean littoral that support the U.S. worldwide military communications system and the collection of electronic intelligence. The region is becoming less important in this respect, however, as advances in technology diminish its geographic advantage. Already, the U.S. Strategic Air Command, which once used airfields in Libya, Morocco, and Saudi Arabia, is no longer a tenant in the Middle East; intermediate-range ballistic missiles are no longer deployed in Turkey; and the importance of the radar sites has declined with improvements in satellite-based intelligence systems. Finally, longer-range submarine-launched missiles and the 1972 treaty limiting the deployment of antiballistic missiles detract from the significance of the Mediterranean for strategic submarine deployments.

The Soviet military presence in the Middle East is more recent than that of the United States. However, Russian concern about developments in the region considerably predates actual deployment of forces. Soviet economic aid and military assistance to the noncommunist world, which began in 1954, has focused intensively on the area. More than 75 percent of Soviet economic credits and grants and an astonishing 80 percent of Soviet military assistance to noncommunist countries have gone to a small group of nations in the Near East and South Asia.[1]

Soviet military forces were not present in the region on a sustained basis until the mid-sixties. Continuous Soviet warship deployments to

1. Reported in U.S. Department of State, "Communist States and Developing Countries: Aid and Trade in 1972," News Release, June 15, 1973.

the Mediterranean began after 1964 and grew significantly only after mid-1967; since then, they have more than doubled. Generally, the reason for Soviet involvement has been strategic defense: a Soviet military presence is intended to deter and, if necessary, to blunt any attack on the Soviet homeland originating from the region; and also to provide a political checkmate to U.S. forces and to inhibit Western intervention. Unlike the U.S. Sixth Fleet, which is primarily oriented toward the projection of land and airpower ashore, the Soviet fleet is mainly designed to counter other naval forces. Soviet emphasis on surface-to-surface cruise missiles supports this contention; so do design features of its warships, its relatively large number of deployed submarines, and the tactical deployments and activity of Soviet naval vessels (for example, in "marking" U.S. carriers) in the Mediterranean. While the Soviet fleet may be viewed by Soviet leaders as a deterrent to—or a means of combating—U.S. intervention in the Mediterranean region, its own interventionary capabilities are quite limited. This is due to such factors as lack of sea-based airpower and the small size of Soviet amphibious forces and naval infantry.

The proposal contained in appendix B, although designed for the Indian Ocean, would be appropriate for a disengagement agreement that covered the entire Mediterranean. There is, however, one complicating factor. The military balance in the Mediterranean, as in most regions, cannot be broken down into separate components; it results synergistically from the interaction between different types of forces. This is particularly so in a relatively narrow sea, where ground-based forces can interact with naval forces, as well as exert an independent influence on the outcome of potential conflicts. For example, until Soviet military units were expelled from Egypt in July 1972, the greatest potential threat to the U.S. Sixth Fleet originated not with the Soviet Mediterranean naval squadron, but with Soviet aircraft carrying cruise missiles based in Egypt. Similarly in 1969 and 1970 Israel viewed the Sixth Fleet primarily as a political counterweight to the deployment of Soviet ground units in Egypt. As a third example, the Soviet Union can be expected to look skeptically at any agreement that bars its naval forces from the Mediterranean but permits the United States to maintain tactical fighter aircraft in Turkey. Thus, in the Mediterranean context, it may be desirable to expand the scope of a disengagement agreement to prohibit the deployment of U.S. and Soviet ground-based units to littoral nations.

Such a clause is, therefore, included in the draft agreement in appendix B. It bars all U.S. and Soviet military forces and installations, with the exception of defense attachés and a limited number of personnel associated with military equipment sales or aid programs, from a specified zone. The most difficult part of the negotiations will be defining the zone from which ground units are to be excluded. The disposition of U.S. forces and bases in Spain, Italy, Greece, and Turkey would present a serious complication for the United States, if the zone were extended beyond the southern and eastern littorals of the Mediterranean. And the Soviet Union might not wish to see its ground-based units permanently barred from Egypt and Syria.

Because the Mediterranean is surrounded by land areas, verification of continued compliance with a naval disengagement agreement would not pose difficult problems. While the deployment of surface vessels can be monitored fairly easily through satellite or aircraft reconnaissance, compliance in regard to submarine deployment is dependent upon the topographic, hydrographic, and other characteristics of the region that determine the effectiveness with which submarine detection systems can be operated.

Once submarines have entered the Mediterranean, in fact, they are very hard to locate. The hydrographic conditions are poor and there is an enormous volume of surface traffic, which makes the detection of submarines by sonars—the primary system—difficult. Nonetheless, there are only three entrances to the Mediterranean—the Turkish Straits, the Strait of Gibraltar, and the Suez Canal. Each of these is quite narrow and submarines are likely to avoid making submerged transits through any but the Gilbraltar passage. The Canal is too shallow, and submerged transit through the Turkish Straits is both prohibited by the Montreux convention and made difficult by the heavy traffic in the waterway. Thus the entrance and exit of submarines from the region can be easily monitored. U.S. capabilities in this regard could be improved by using ground-based systems in Turkey and Spain. While the Soviets are unlikely to be granted similar facilities, they do not need to be concerned with the Turkish Straits and maintenance of Soviet naval vessels near the western entrance to the Mediterranean should make them relatively confident of verifying U.S. compliance.

The crucial question from the U.S. perspective is whether in terms of overall policy the country has more to gain or more to lose from naval disengagement in the Mediterranean. An agreement on the lines described in chapter 4 indicates such a complex pattern of likely advantages and disadvantages, potential risks and benefits, that it is difficult to evaluate its effect in any rigorous or systematic manner.

Potential Benefits for the United States

The most immediate and direct benefits of Mediterranean disengagement would be those associated with the tactical military situation. In the Mediterranean, two large and technologically sophisticated fleets confront one another on a daily basis. Both surface units are vulnerable to a surprise attack and therefore each has to remain constantly on alert. Moreover, they operate in a region beset with chronic instabilities and frequent local conflicts, a region lacking commonly recognized boundaries of the superpowers' vital interests.

Neither the United States nor the Soviet Union can be certain of its rival's intentions in the Middle East; nor what the other will do when the region is torn by one of its recurring crises. Such uncertainty threatens to turn any conflict of purely local significance into one of global dimensions.

Both the United States and the Soviet Union showed how aware they were of these dangers when they concluded the agreement on the prevention of incidents involving warships in 1972.[2] This treaty (signed by former U.S. Secretary of the Navy John W. Warner and Commander-in-Chief of the Soviet Navy Sergei G. Gorshkov) is important because it reduces the possibility of accidents and harassment incidents by the rival military units. But it does not get to the heart of the problem— the danger of involvement, accidentally or through miscalculation, on opposing sides in local conflicts. In essence, the Warner-Gorshkov agreement simply pledged each side to abide by long-standing "rules of the road" governing the activities of naval vessels on the high seas. A more durable and far-reaching agreement requires fundamental political decisions in Moscow and Washington.

2. Agreement between the Government of the United States of America and the Government of the Union of Soviet Socialist Republics on the Prevention of Incidents on and over the High Seas, signed May 25, 1972, at Moscow. See U.S. Department of State, *United States Treaties and Other International Agreements* (Washington, D.C.: Government Printing Office, 1972), vol. 23, pt. 1, pp. 1168–74.

A disengagement agreement would reduce the risk of inadvertent conflict between the two Mediterranean fleets. The physical disentanglement of the two navies would diminish tension, lead to fewer incidents, and lessen the risk of preemptive action in time of crisis. While securing these mutual U.S.–Soviet benefits, the agreement would also improve the military disposition of U.S. forces in the Middle East. For some time, fears have been expressed that the U.S. Sixth Fleet, as presently deployed and operated, is in an untenable military situation. Since the Mediterranean constitutes a relatively confined space, and since modern reconnaissance technology is quite advanced, it can be assumed that the location of major elements of the Sixth Fleet are known by the Soviet Union, with some precision most of the time. During crises in the Middle East (precisely the time when the outbreak of U.S.–Soviet conflict is most likely) the fleet tends to move eastward to demonstrate U.S. resolve and to warn potential opponents. At such times, the Sixth Fleet is within range of Soviet aircraft carrying cruise missiles based within the USSR (the situation would be even worse if Soviet forces regained Egyptian bases or a local alternative). Cruise missiles constitute a serious threat to naval vessels. This certainly is the case when armed with nuclear warheads and may also be true even when armed with conventional munitions. Additionally, the Soviet Union could at any time use submarines. The nine Soviet submarines typically deployed in the Mediterranean, some of which are armed with subsurface-to-surface cruise missiles in addition to torpedoes, could inflict considerable damage to the Sixth Fleet.

If the fleet were deployed outside the Mediterranean except for intermittent cruises, it would be beyond the range of most Soviet land-based aircraft and its precise whereabouts in the Atlantic might be somewhat less certain for longer periods of time. Should the agreement break down for any reason, the fleet could be returned to the Mediterranean; if need be, after first clearing the region of enemy surface and submarine units using land-based aircraft. Thus, by reducing the Sixth Fleet's vulnerability to a preemptive strike, the agreement could actually increase the force's potential military utility. At the same time, the agreement would shift the military balance in a way that would not be possible by any other means short of war—a reversal of the Soviet military buildup in the Middle East since the mid-sixties.

Soviet naval deployments to the Mediterranean Sea (described in appendix A) have grown significantly since 1967. Although their military presence ashore has not kept pace, there have been recurring reports of Soviet attempts to acquire naval facilities in several nations. The consequences of this buildup have been, and are likely to continue to be, largely political. For one thing, Soviet growth brings into question U.S. willingness to intervene in future Middle East crises, and this could encourage the Arab states to adopt a more hostile stance vis-à-vis Israel. For another, the increasing size of the Soviet Mediterranean fleet is viewed with some trepidation by U.S. allies in Europe: an incipient threat to NATO's southern flank, the supply lines to Greece and Turkey in the event of war, and the shipment of petroleum from the Persian Gulf and North Africa to Europe. As the initial Soviet buildup occurred simultaneously with a small decline in the size of the U.S. fleet in the Mediterranean—caused by the advancing age of U.S. ships and by requirements for U.S. forces in Southeast Asia—the military balance in the region appeared to be changing quite rapidly. Some NATO members have feared that the balance was being permanently altered, and that the United States was no longer able, or simply unwilling, to provide the resources necessary to deter Soviet expansion.

Mutual U.S.–Soviet naval disengagement offers a low-cost, low-risk strategy for terminating these trends in the military balance. The alternative strategy would be for the United States to deploy additional forces to the region. While this might offset the political consequences, it would be costly and, more important, it would probably lead to further Soviet deployments and a spiraling naval race in the region.

In broader terms, superpower military disengagement in the Mediterranean Sea would tend to depolarize intraregional conflicts. It would lessen, for example, the rigidity of the U.S.–Soviet positions on Israel and the Arab states, and would serve notice on local regimes that the superpowers were intent on avoiding direct involvement in regional disputes. This could be a significant development. The superpowers are not likely—even without a disengagement agreement—to interfere at the onset of a Middle Eastern conflict, but the probability of their intervention at a later stage is not negligible. The gradual involvement of Soviet military units in fighting along the Suez Canal during 1969 and 1970 provides an excellent example; so do the U.S. and Soviet naval buildups in connection with the 1970 Jordanian crisis and the 1973 Arab-Israeli war.

In effect, by agreeing to limit the deployment of military forces to the Middle East, the two superpowers would be reducing the importance of these forces as a means of enhancing their respective influence in the region. This would give weight, at the most dangerous point on the globe, to the principles agreed to by President Nixon and General Secretary Brezhnev at their first Moscow summit:

The U.S.A. and the U.S.S.R. attach major importance to preventing the development of situations capable of causing a dangerous exacerbation of their relations. Therefore, they will seek to promote conditions in which all countries will live in peace and security and will not be subject to outside interference in their internal affairs.[3]

Potential Risks for the United States

Naval disengagement in the Mediterranean also implies some risk with regard to U.S. strategic capabilities, U.S. relations with some of its allies, and the flexibility of U.S. policy in the event of certain contingencies.

Strategic risks

The United States now deploys strategic ballistic missile submarines (SSBNs) in the Mediterranean. Under the proposed disengagement regime, these deployments would have to be forgone. This would not significantly affect U.S. strategic capabilities at present and is likely to have even less effect in the future. When SSBNs were first deployed in the Mediterranean during the early sixties the range of missiles was limited. Deploying strategic submarines to the eastern Mediterranean brought new regions of the Soviet Union within reach of U.S. sea-based missiles for the first time. In effect, Polaris SSBN patrols in the Mediterranean substituted for the vulnerable land-based, intermediate-range ballistic missiles then being withdrawn from Turkey. The range of sea-based ballistic missiles has doubled since that time, however, and the value of the region for this purpose has declined commensurately. By 1980,

---

3. "Basic Principles of Mutual Relations between the United States of America and the Union of Soviet Socialist Republics," signed May 29, 1972, at Moscow. See U.S. Department of State, *Bulletin*, vol. 66, no. 1722 (June 26, 1972), pp. 898–99.

Table 4-1. Range of Submarine-Launched Ballistic Missiles and Distance between Selected Soviet Cities and Hypothetical Launch Points

Missile	Year of initial operating capability	Range (nautical miles)
Polaris A-1	1960	1,200
Polaris A-2	1962	1,500
Polaris A-3	1964	2,500
Poseidon	1971	2,500
Trident I	1978[a]	4,500
Trident II	1982[a]	6,000

City	Distance between launch point and selected Soviet cities (nautical miles)	
	Mediterranean[b]	Atlantic[c]
Odessa	700	3,200
Kiev	800	3,100
Volgograd	1,100	3,700
Moscow	1,600	3,300
Sverdlovsk	1,900	3,900
Tashkent	1,900	4,800

Sources: Missile characteristics: R. T. Pretty and D. H. R. Archer (eds.), *Jane's Weapon Systems, 1970/71* (Sampson Low, 1970), and International Institute for Strategic Studies, *The Military Balance, 1972/73* (London: International Institute, 1972). Distances: author's estimates that represent great circle map distances (the actual length of the missile's trajectory would also be influenced by the earth's rotation during its flight).
a. Estimated.
b. Launch point taken at 35° N, 30° E.
c. Launch point taken at 40° N, 45° W.

when the new Trident submarine with its even longer-range missiles becomes operational, targets now assigned to submarines in the Mediterranean will be vulnerable to boats cruising in the mid-Atlantic (Table 4-1).

Effect on U.S.–Allied Relations

Third nations could play a major, if negative, role in influencing the outcome of a disengagement proposal from both the U.S. and Soviet viewpoints. While it is doubtful that either superpower could be sufficiently encouraged by outside views to accept an agreement that it might otherwise reject as being, in net terms, against the national interest, third nations—if they expressed considerable hostility—might be able to forestall agreement. In this regard, the views of all nations would be considered, but both the United States and the USSR would be most concerned with the opinions of their allies and client states; strongly negative reactions on their part could be perceived by the superpowers as overriding any potential benefits of the agreement. For example, disengagement in the Mediterranean could have serious negative repercussions in U.S.–Israeli relations (a subject discussed later in the chapter); and the impact on Western Europe is difficult to predict.

REACTIONS IN EUROPE. In one sense, naval disengagement would be evaluated favorably by Western Europe because it implies that Europe will not be so closely linked to U.S. policy in the Middle East. This has been an important objective of most nations in Western Europe since 1967, and particularly since the 1973–74 oil embargo and production cutback. The primary symbol representing both the U.S. commitment to Israel and the U.S. posture in Europe is the Sixth Fleet. Removal of the fleet would visibly weaken this connection.

Additionally, some nations in Europe see broader advantages in curbing the superpower military presence in the Mediterranean. France, Italy, and Spain have a special interest in avoiding conflict in the region. Moreover, they have the most to gain from closer ties between Western Europe and the nations on the eastern and southern littorals of the Mediterranean. They are more dependent upon these states for oil imports than the northern European nations and have developed mutually beneficial trade, financial, and population exchanges with many south Mediterranean nations.[4]

France has been a vigorous supporter of superpower disengagement in the Mediterranean for some time, as such measures dovetail neatly with the general thrust of French foreign policy since the early 1960s. Interestingly, one of General Charles de Gaulle's first steps toward reducing French participation in NATO was to withdraw the French fleet from joint NATO command. Former President Georges Pompidou continued his predecessor's policies and, on several occasions, expressed France's desire "to remove the Mediterranean from the great nuclear powers' struggle."[5]

Spanish and Italian interests in Mediterranean disengagement have

4. There has been considerable interest lately in the development of closer ties between the northern and southern Mediterranean littorals; see Jon McLin, "The European Community and the Mediterranean: Co-Prosperity Sphere or North-South Confrontation Zone," *American Universities Fieldstaff Reports*, West Europe Series, 8 (April 1973).

5. Paris Domestic Service; reported in FBIS, *Daily Report: Western Europe*, January 22, 1971.

been more closely associated with particular political leaders or factions than in the French case. Spain's former foreign minister, Fernando Maria Castiella y Mais, was an outspoken advocate of disengagement and was reported on November 19, 1968, to have urged such a course directly to Secretary of State Dean Rusk.[6] Italy's position was most closely associated with former Premier Emilio Colombo. Unlike Castiella y Mais, Colombo's support for disengagement was indirect and phrased in terms of generally improving the prospects for peace in the region.[7]

The effect of recent political changes in these three nations on their views toward disengagement remains to be seen. In any case, however, certain other U.S. allies in Europe are unlikely to favor naval disengagement in the Mediterranean. Two sorts of considerations would lead to negative reactions.

The first relates to projections of the tactical military situation following a naval disengagement agreement. If U.S. forces left the Mediterranean (along with Soviet forces), and if the Soviet Union later staged a sudden military offensive against NATO countries, the United States would have to inject externally based forces through a relatively narrow chokepoint (the Strait of Gibraltar) in order to return. The USSR could attempt to deny such entry and, given specific tactical advantages on their side, might be successful. Although the relative inefficiencies of having the Sixth Fleet caught by surprise attack while in the Mediterranean and having it so disposed that it had to fight its way back into the Mediterranean after the opening of hostilities are not obvious, such considerations might cause concern to states on NATO's southern flank—Greece and Turkey. Assuming that the present difficulties between the United States and these nations are resolved in such a way that they remain members of the alliance, Greece and Turkey might question the strength of U.S. commitments when faced with the choice between reaching a settlement with the USSR and having its fleet fight its way back into the Mediterranean. Greece and Turkey might then reevaluate their relations with the United States and the Soviet Union. Of course, staging a surprise offensive in an age of satel-

6. Reported in *New York Times* (November 21, 1968) and *Atlantic*, vol. 225 (February 1970), p. 14. Spain's interest, however, may have been designed primarily for leverage during renegotiation of the agreement governing U.S. military bases in Spain.

7. See, for example, an interview with Premier Colombo on Belgrade TANJUG Domestic Service; reported in FBIS, *Daily Report: Western Europe*, March 24, 1971.

lite and electronic reconnaissance would be difficult and the relative military advantages of the two dispositions are not evident. Nonetheless, political relations between states are founded only loosely on objective military considerations, and therefore fears of weakening U.S. resolve following a disengagement could well have negative political consequences.

Other considerations likely to influence U.S. allies are even less tangible. Some European states tend to believe that any reduction in U.S. military deployments overseas indicates lessening U.S. commitment to their defense. Thus a wider group of allies—and especially Germany—might view the Mediterranean disengagement agreement as foreshadowing a U.S. intent to leave Europe, and as another sign of growing isolationist sentiment. It would be argued by some in Europe (as well as by American critics of any proposed agreement) that adherence to the treaty implied U.S. desertion of its NATO allies on the southern flank. The point that the agreement would also remove Soviet forces would be dismissed because of Soviet propinquity. The argument would continue that the United States might then take similar actions on NATO's central front and that it would be prudent for the states of Western Europe to reexamine their security plans and policies in this light. The degree to which such sentiment might affect policy decisions in Germany and other European states is unclear.

REACTIONS IN ISRAEL. At the present time, Israel would also oppose naval disengagement in the Mediterranean. Israel's reaction might have been different before the 1973 war, when Israelis were confident of their enduring military superiority over the bordering Arab states. With such a perception, Israel favored, and primarily exercised, self-reliance in its defense policies, depending on the United States only for the supply of military equipment. For example, in 1969, when a reporter put the following question to General Haim Bar-Lev, chief of the Israeli General Staff: "Let me suggest for a moment, that there were no Sixth Fleet, no Soviet Fleet in the Mediterranean. How would this affect the situation in the Middle East?" the general replied directly:

> Well I am sure the situation will be much easier and we could be much closer to a settlement without the Soviet presence here and without the American Sixth Fleet.[8]

The 1973 war, however, altered Israeli views profoundly. While Israel was on the verge of winning that conflict in a military sense when

8. "Russia in the Mediterranean," *NBC News Special*, March 16, 1969; transcript, p. 18.

the cease-fire was concluded, serious setbacks during the early course of the fighting and the high casualty and equipment-loss rates made more real to Israelis the prospect that they might not retain their military superiority indefinitely. Thus Israelis now value more highly the U.S. commitment to their defense, and the Sixth Fleet in the Mediterranean is the most tangible symbol of that commitment.

A physical U.S. presence in the region is particularly important to Israel because its leaders have long believed that no nation will willingly help, once push really comes to shove. This distrust has been reinforced by several incidents—U.S. pressures on Israel to withdraw from Sinai in 1957, pressures for partial Israeli withdrawals from occupied territory in 1974, and U.S. vacillation following closure of the Strait of Tiran in 1967 and during Soviet-Egyptian violations of the cease-fire accord reached in 1970. Israel's anxiety is intensified by increasing U.S. dependence on Arab oil. It could therefore be expected to resist vigorously what it regarded as further erosion of U.S. pledges, such as the withdrawal of the Sixth Fleet from the Mediterranean.

Effect on the Flexibility of U.S. Foreign Policy

Adherence to a disengagement regime would imply a downgrading of the role of military force in U.S. dealings with Mediterranean states. With the escape clauses and the provision for emergency deployments this shift would not be irreversible, but it would compound the problems of staging sizable military operations. Consequently, one would expect the United States to resort less frequently to military demonstrations. Although the long-term net effectiveness of such measures (for example, show-the-flag cruises, shows of force, military interventions) are the subject of considerable debate, they are often used and are sometimes effective—at least in the short run—in influencing the outcome of certain events. A disengagement agreement might make it more difficult for future presidents to use these options.

Concern in this respect focuses most pointedly on contingencies involving Israel. As was made so evident during the fall of 1973, U.S. intervention in an Arab-Israeli war is not a remote possibility; particularly if it is required to deter or counter Soviet intervention. Even if U.S. combat involvement in Arab-Israeli fighting does not take place, U.S. naval forces in the Mediterranean can expedite the delivery of arms and supplies to Israel and possibly interrupt Soviet shipments to the Arabs. And during peacetime and crises, the presence of the Sixth Fleet constitutes a visible reminder to the Soviets of the risks they would run should they contemplate injecting their own forces into a future Arab-Israeli war.

In evaluating Mediterranean naval disengagement, one must consider the potential effects of downgrading the U.S. military presence on the perceptions and actions of decisionmakers in Israel and the Arab states. Would attainment of such an agreement encourage the Arabs to renew open hostilities or to adopt a more rigid posture at the peace talks? Would it tend to reduce the U.S. ability to lead Israel toward concessions in the negotiations? Would it encourage Israel to develop nuclear weapons? There are no simple answers to these questions, and none are suggested here. Judgments must be reached, however, before one could either endorse or oppose a proposed disengagement agreement.

Mediterranean Disengagement from the Soviet Perspective

The Soviet Union, of course, shares many of the same benefits from an agreement of this type as the United States—reduced risk of inadvertent conflict between the two fleets, the positive contribution of naval disengagement in the settlement of local conflicts, the greater likelihood of additional agreements between the superpowers.

The proposed agreement also provides some benefits that Soviet decisionmakers might consider favor the USSR more than the United States. It publicly, and explicitly, reaffirms a basic implication of the agreements resulting from the first round of strategic arms limitation talks—that the USSR is a great power second to none, the military equal of the United States. Achievement of such status has been a long-standing goal of Soviet policy, important for Soviet prestige, and of benefit to the USSR in future dealings with the United States and other nations.

Moreover, Soviet leaders probably evaluate the military concessions granted by the United States as greater than those yielded by the USSR. While the United States would yield a strategic threat to the Soviet homeland, the USSR would yield only a first-strike threat to the Sixth Fleet; Soviet Mediterranean forces have no capability to strike the United States itself. While the United States would withdraw a force with designated missions in support of NATO ground forces, the Soviet fleet has only a derivative role in the defense of the Warsaw Pact countries. While the United States would reduce its ability to apply pressure close to Soviet borders, the USSR would yield only rights far from American shores. While the United States would withdraw a force capable of intervention against armed opposition anywhere on the Mediterranean littoral, the USSR would withdraw a force capable of intervention only from secure friendly territory. Generally, the United States would remove a more capable naval force and a more extensive shore-based infrastructure, with the ratio of withdrawals, as indexed by manpower, likely to be as high as two to one.

On the other hand, the consequences of the proposed agreement for the tactical naval situation would not be wholly clear to Soviet decisionmakers. When Soviet naval strategists no longer needed to consider maintaining a large standing naval force in the Mediterranean, they would have greater flexibility and more Soviet vessels available for service elsewhere. Additionally, the Soviet surface fleet would be less vulnerable to a preemptive first strike by the United States. Nonetheless, the USSR would recognize that the Sixth Fleet also would be less vulnerable than before and that, while the agreement would have reduced the psychological-political impact of the fleet's physical presence, it would probably also improve the force's war-fighting capability. More important, in examining their options should the treaty break down suddenly, Soviet decisionmakers would have to view the prospect of the Soviet Navy fighting its way in through narrow straits controlled by Spain and Turkey—two nations which, from their perspective, at best would be neutral in any U.S.–Soviet confrontation.

The Soviet Union would also have to consider the implications for its relations with the Arab states. It would no doubt claim credit for the removal of U.S. naval forces, thus blunting a latent threat to Arab nationalism and removing the primary U.S. support for Israel. This would fit well with increasing emphasis on the role of the Soviet Navy as an instrument for deterring Western intervention in the nonaligned world. At the same time, although the United States would surrender the greater force potential in crises, it is the USSR that would probably have greater incentive to intervene in the years to come. At least for the near term, if open hostilities in the Middle East recur, the military weakness of Egypt and Syria relative to Israel is more likely to find the Soviet Union, rather than the United States, with cause to use military force on behalf of its clients. Under the terms of the agreement, these operations would be made more difficult.

Egypt and Syria have both welcomed the deployment of the Soviet fleet in the Mediterranean, believing that the Soviet presence helps to deter potential American military involvement in the Middle East. The Soviet fleet is believed to restrain not only potential American support for Israel, but also American intervention in defense of conservative Arab regimes—such as Lebanon in 1958. Thus Egypt and Syria perceive that the Soviet naval presence has given them greater flexibility in their policies toward Israel, placed them under less pressure to reach an unfavorable peace settlement, and generally permitted them to exercise greater independence in their foreign affairs. For example, an editorial in Cairo's *Egyptian Gazette* noted:

> Soviet naval units in the Mediterranean . . . are there to see to it that the Mediterranean does not in fact become an American lake under the control of the U.S. Sixth Fleet. . . . It is for this reason that President Abdan-Nasir proclaimed: "I say that all free countries of the area welcome the presence of the Soviet fleet in the Mediterranean."[9]

There is, however, reason to question whether this logic would necessarily lead to an adverse reaction if there were a serious prospect of superpower naval disengagement. For one thing, sophisticated Arab observers may suspect Soviet willingness to confront the United States in situations involving a high risk of conflict. Most examples of the USSR's use of its Navy as an instrument of suasion have generally been marginal cases with regard to the risk of American involvement.[10] With the exception of arms shipments, the Soviet *naval* presence certainly was of little benefit to Egypt or Syria during the 1967 Six-Day War, the 1970 Jordanian crisis, or the 1973 war.[11] While the USSR reinforced its naval forces during each of these crises, there is some evidence that Soviet units avoided indicating hostile intent toward the Sixth Fleet and that Soviet and American leaders remained in frequent contact so as to minimize the risk of a military confrontation. Thus a disengagement agreement that removed the Sixth Fleet from the Mediterranean, even at the price of the Soviet presence, could well appear preferable to Egypt and Syria, compared to the present situation in which both navies maintain large standing deployments. In the end, their assessment is

---

9. *Egyptian Gazette*, July 25, 1968; English translation.

10. For example, Ghana (1969), Somalia (1969 and 1970), Guinea (1971), Iraq (1973). See Robert G. Weinland, "Soviet Naval Operations—Ten Years of Change," Professional Paper 125 (Arlington, Va.: Center for Naval Analyses, 1974).

11. In the last case, however, the threat of a Soviet intervention using airborne troops may have been an important factor in causing the United States to pressure Israel to abide by the second cease-fire.

likely to depend on three determinants: projections of the future Arab-Israeli military balance; assessments of Soviet willingness to confront the United States in a future crisis; and forecasts of the strength of U.S. commitments to Israel.

There are now pressures from Arab sources for support of measures to reduce the superpower naval presence in the Mediterranean. Although the degree to which Egypt and Syria depend upon Soviet military support belies the precepts of "nonalignment," such notions should not be considered empty phrases. A desire for complete independence from great power influence may be downplayed at present in light of real-world difficulties (such as Israel's superior military capabilities), but it remains a salient long-range objective of the Arab states. This is partly because many leaders within the nonaligned world—Algeria's Boumédienne, Yugoslavia's Tito, Libya's Qaadhaffi, and others—who could exercise some influence in the ultimate evaluations of Syria and Egypt, have been vigorous supporters of naval disengagement.

Hard evidence on the present attitudes of Egypt and Syria are scarce, but there seems to have been some movement in favor of disengagement since 1972. Before that time both states carefully resisted making favorable statements. Thus communiqués and speeches issued during Boumédienne's visits to Syria in 1970 differed considerably from those issued during his visits to Libya, Tunisia, Saudi Arabia, and European nations during roughly the same period. Whereas the latter communications tended to call explicitly for removal of the two superpower navies from the Mediterranean, statements issued during the Syrian visit spoke only of "removing all causes of military tension."[12]

The turning point seems to have been the expulsion of Soviet military units from Egypt in July 1972. Since that time various statements supporting "neutralization" of the Mediterranean have appeared in the Egyptian media.[13] And Egypt supported the call for superpower disengagement in the Mediterranean issued at the Algiers conference of nonaligned nations.[14] Thus Egypt's reduced dependence on the USSR for military support and its improved relations with the United States may have bolstered its confidence that Egyptian interests would be served by a "neutralized" Mediterranean.

12. Algiers Domestic Service in Arabic, February 6, 1970; English translation.
13. See, for example, the report of the Cairo Domestic Service, September 24, 1972; English translation.
14. Reported in *New York Times*, August 29, 1972.

CHAPTER FIVE

DISENGAGEMENT IN THE INDIAN OCEAN

Until recently, the two superpowers exercised relative restraint in their naval deployments to the Indian Ocean.[1] Warships of the Soviet Union did not enter the region until 1968; their combatant presence there remains relatively small. Although the United States has maintained a three-ship naval force in the region since the late 1940s, it only began to deploy major task forces (with the exception of infrequent transits, exercises, and the 1971 Indian-Pakistani crisis) following the 1973 war in the Middle East. But by late 1974 the two nations were entering the early stages of a buildup in the area. They each had increased the number of warships typically deployed there, and each has during the last year taken steps to establish a more permanent presence. The U.S. Department of State requested authorization from Congress to expand naval and aircraft support facilities on the island of Diego Garcia. And in July 1974, the Soviet Union concluded a treaty of friendship and cooperation with the Democratic Republic of Somalia; U.S. military officials report that Somalia has granted various basing rights to the USSR.[2]

1. U.S. and Soviet naval activities in the Indian Ocean are described in appendix A.
2. The Soviet Union has signed similar treaties with Egypt, India, and Iraq in recent years. Interestingly enough, in these earlier instances the text of the agreement was published nearly simultaneously with the announcement of the signing; the text of the Somali treaty was not made public until four months after its ratification (*Pravda*, October 30, 1974; reported in FBIS, *Daily Report: Soviet Union*, November 1, 1974). Article 4 of the treaty states ". . . the high contracting parties will continue to develop cooperation in the military sphere on the basis of the corresponding agreements between them." Testimony by U.S. Navy officials on the Soviet military presence in Somalia is given in *Military Procurement Supplemental—Fiscal Year 1974*, Hearings before the Senate Committee on Armed Services, 93 Cong. 2 sess. (1974), pp. 46–47. A less alarming view was given by Director William E. Colby of the Central Intelligence Agency in *Military Con-*

Nonetheless, because naval competition in the Indian Ocean is still in an early phase, and because of other factors to be described later, the prospect for negotiation of a disengagement regime is probably greater for the Indian Ocean than for the Mediterranean. At the same time, the potential benefits of such an agreement are not as great as they are in the Mediterranean. The Indian Ocean is not a confined sea and the United States and the Soviet Union maintain smaller naval forces there on a day-to-day basis. Moreover, at least until early 1975, situations in which the superpowers felt compelled to augment their naval presence have developed far less often. Consequently, the risk of inadvertent conflict between the superpowers growing out of a crisis-related naval confrontation—avoidance of which is an important benefit of Mediter-ranean disengagement—is not as great. Similarly, other potential bene-fits of Mediterranean disengagement, such as the possible depolarization of local conflicts and the promotion of better relations between the United States and the USSR, are not likely to be as significant in the case of the Indian Ocean.

The potential benefit of Indian Ocean naval disengagement is, in fact, to avoid a situation developing that might eventually become as critical as the one now existing in the Mediterranean. Aside from the momen-tum of the naval buildup already in progress, several considerations are propelling both superpowers into an even larger effort in the Indian Ocean.

On the U.S. side, the use of military force is being discussed as a possible counterstrategy in the event of an embargo by the oil-producing states on the Persian Gulf. Moreover, the fact that effects of the 1973 Middle East war spilled over into the Indian Ocean because of a block-ade at the Bab-al-Mandeb (the entrance to the Red Sea) and naval operations in adjoining waters, may mean that the United States will look favorably upon an enlarged naval presence in the Indian Ocean in anticipation of future Arab-Israeli conflict. (Other factors prompting U.S. deployments are discussed below.)

On the Soviet side, the reopening of the Suez Canal will increase the rapidity with which the USSR could reinforce its naval forces in the Indian Ocean at times of crisis and reduce the cost of maintaining a

---

struction Authorization, Fiscal Year 1975, Hearings before the Subcommittee on Military Construction of the Senate Committee on Armed Services (1974), 93 Cong. 2 sess. (1974), pp. 161–72.

standing naval force in the region during peacetime. Thus with the Canal in use both temporary and permanent deployments would be more attractive from the Soviet viewpoint. Soviet decisionmakers have also to consider the possibility that an enhanced naval presence would not only indicate Soviet support of friendly states, notably India, but also check China's influence in the region by serving as a counter to any expansion in Chinese naval capabilities: considerations not foreign to decisionmakers in the United States.

In any event, each superpower is likely to look upon any further increase in its rival's naval presence in the Indian Ocean—no matter what the cause—as an incentive to step up its own naval activity. Thus it is not unreasonable to project continuing increases in both U.S. and Soviet deployments to the region. A U.S.–USSR naval disengagement, such as the one outlined in appendix B, offers the prospect of reversing this buildup, thereby reducing the risk of direct superpower conflict or combatant involvement in local disputes and thereby avoiding other costs.

The key question is whether potential benefits are sufficient to outweigh considerations prompting the deployments. Many disparate elements enter into the calculation. The Indian Ocean is large and bordered by many states that may be combined in several relatively autonomous subregions. Each subregion—the African Coast, the Persian Gulf, South Asia, Southeast Asia—raises different issues in regard to disengagement, and each is affected by different external relationships. A few of the more important considerations are discussed below.

1. General political benefits of a naval presence. Maintenance of a standing naval presence in particular regions, even in the absence of demonstrative actions by the force, is more and more viewed in both the United States and the Soviet Union as a useful way of supporting foreign policy objectives. Such a fleet serves some operational purposes: it permits the deploying power to respond more promptly to crises; it provides operational experience on the scene for local commanders; and it facilitates arrangements for communications, intelligence, replenishment, and the like. The more important reasons, though, are intangible— a perceived diffuse political advantage. It is believed that a naval presence sensitizes local nations to the possible consequences of their own decisions on superpower objectives. The deployments are a visible reminder of U.S. or Soviet military power and superpower interest in the area, and they are an implicit threat of superpower involvement in local affairs should events proceed in an adverse fashion.

Even though the manner in which a naval presence enhances super-power influence in an area is poorly understood, some officials in both the United States and the Soviet Union would argue against naval disengagement agreements on this basis. Disengagement in the Indian Ocean, moreover, raises special issues. For example, recent attention paid to the region's oil resources have emphasized the presumed usefulness of a naval presence in influencing decisions by local governments.

2. China. The People's Republic of China has made no secret of its pleasure in seeing the United States provide a military counterweight to Soviet deployments in the Indian Ocean; a fact the USSR is fond of publicizing. Because they do not presently have the capability of deploying a credible military force of their own to the region, the Chinese seem content to pursue the traditional practice of playing one "barbarian" off against the other. Should both barbarians withdraw from the region, the Chinese Navy at some point in the future might play a significant role. To the extent that this is considered undesirable, it is one possible disadvantage of Indian Ocean disengagement.

This consideration is more important for the Soviet Union than for the United States. Soviet deployments to the Indian Ocean could well stem primarily from concern over China. In the event of a Sino-Soviet war, the Indian Ocean would provide an important logistical route for the shipment of supplies to Soviet military forces in the Far East. More to the point, perhaps, Soviet peacetime naval deployments to the region help to bolster India's position as a possible foe of the Chinese. Soviet naval activity is a tangible reminder of close Soviet-Indian relations, thereby encouraging India's resistance to Chinese encroachments. In the event of a new Sino-Indian conflict, the Soviet naval presence could figure in the military balance in a more direct manner. Soviet decision-makers might thus be concerned about the effect of disengagement on Indian perceptions of the future naval balance in the region.

3. The Persian Gulf. Two considerations are important: which country is likely to dominate this subregion if the United States and the Soviet Union withdraw their fleets, and the possible utility of military force in the present oil situation.

The first consideration again poses difficulties mainly for the Soviet Union. Although there seems little doubt that Iran is now the dominant military power on the Gulf, a disengagement agreement, by removing other naval forces from the region, would enable Iran to dominate the Persian Gulf and adjoining waters even more effectively. That is why the Shah has made no secret that he favors the removal of both U.S.

and Soviet naval forces.[3] He reasons that a U.S. naval presence in the Persian Gulf helps to justify the deployment of Soviet warships to the region, and that it would be in Iran's interest if both remained outside those confined waters.

The Soviet problem arises from its close relationship with Iraq—a state that has been in military conflict with Iran over a number of issues—and, more generally, its support of revolutionary movements in the sheikhdoms along the Gulf. In effect, a Soviet naval withdrawal from the region could be interpreted by these clients as evidence of Soviet unwillingness to oppose Iran's quest for dominance in the Gulf—an evaluation that the USSR would not wish to encourage.

The oil situation, of course, poses greater difficulties for the United States than for the Soviet Union. One can conceive of three contingencies in which the United States might consider using naval forces in the Indian Ocean because of the oil emergency.

First, under certain conditions, the United States might wish to use naval forces to seize oil fields along the Gulf so as to prevent or to end future oil embargoes. Although such an action is likely to be considered only when an embargo has lasted sufficiently long to cause real economic hardship in this country, and although there is some question whether the long-term costs of such an action might not exceed the potential benefits, the contingency cannot be totally ignored. If nothing else, an implicit threat to carry out a seizure, by maintaining a naval presence, might help to deter a prolonged embargo and cause the oil producers to be more cooperative in terms of the Arab-Israeli conflict, pricing policies, and so forth. Official U.S. interest in naval disengagement in the Indian Ocean might undermine these effects.

Second, less likely but still possible is a scenario in which the United States intervened in the Gulf to prevent the overthrow of the present Saudi Arabian government.

And finally, another, if still remote, possibility is that the United States might wish to use naval forces to escort tankers carrying oil from the Gulf to this country, Japan, or Western Europe.[4]

---

3. See, for example, comments made in response to the announcement of the U.S. intention to take over Britain's base at Bahrain (reported in *New York Times*, January 17, 1972), and comments during the Shah's recent trip to Australia (*New York Times*, September 29, 1974).

4. See Barry M. Blechman and Arnold M. Kuzmack, "Oil and National Security," *Naval War College Review* (May–June 1974), pp. 8–25.

To the degree that one takes these scenarios seriously, they argue against U.S.–Soviet naval disengagement in the Indian Ocean, since the U.S. military potential in each instance would be weakened—although not permanently—by such an agreement.

4. The spillover effect of the Arab-Israeli conflict. The U.S. decision to deploy a carrier task force to the Indian Ocean following the 1973 Arab-Israeli war—and since then to maintain an augmented presence in the region—has never been fully explained. One possible motive was to provide an implicit threat against the states then participating in the oil embargo. This is supported by the observation that the initial task force generally remained near the Saudi coast.[5]

Other explanations focus more closely on the Arab-Israeli conflict. It is possible that the U.S. deployments were intended to threaten the Arab blockade of the Bab-al-Mandeb—the entrance to the Red Sea. An American-owned freighter, the S.S. *La Salle,* flying the Liberian flag, was reported to have been damaged by units participating in the blockade. It was apparently delivering supplies for the Kagnew station just before being fired upon. There are reports also that the Soviet Union provided some support for the blockade.[6] If these are accurate, the U.S. deployments may have been designed both to pressure Egypt to end the blockade and to deter further Soviet involvement. In any case, the option of providing sea-based tactical air support to Israel from the Red Sea might be considered in any future conflict. A disengagement agreement would make such support more difficult.

5. Verification problems. Unlike the Mediterranean, the Indian Ocean is a wide-open body of water. Entry from the Atlantic side can be gained anywhere from Africa to the Antarctic; entry from the Pacific side is possible either through the most common route—the Strait of Malacca—or through a number of straits in the Indonesian archipelago. Consequently it would be difficult to monitor the passage of naval vessels into and out of the region. While this problem poses no difficulty for an agreement restricted to surface ships, which would be visible to satellite reconnaissance, it does argue for the exclusion of submarines. It might be possible to monitor a submarine restriction by tracking all

5. Reported in *Canberra Times*, December 3, 1973.
6. Reported by John M. Gurner, "The Reopening of the Suez: Who Gains? Who Loses?" *U.S. Naval Institute Proceedings* (October 1974), p. 105; see also, Lawrence Whetten and Michael Johnson, "Military Lessons of the Yom Kippur War," *World Today*, vol. 30 (March 1974).

submarines from the time they left their home ports, but neither signatory would have much confidence in such an approach. On the other hand, cheating on the submarine provisions of a disengagement agreement would hardly compensate for the political consequences should the violation be discovered. It is difficult to imagine how any Soviet infringement, even if large numbers of submarines were involved (which, of course, increases the likelihood of discovery), could seriously jeopardize the security interests of the United States. On balance, therefore, it seems desirable to include submarines in any agreement.[7]

   6. SSBN Deployments. U.S. strategic submarines do not regularly patrol the Indian Ocean, but under certain circumstances it might be advantageous to do so. Patrols of strategic ballistic missile submarines (SSBNs) in the Indian Ocean would extend the geographic arc in which the United States threatens the USSR with incoming missiles: a desirable step should the Soviets deploy a major antiballistic missile defense system. Moreover, SSBN deployments to the Indian Ocean would offer a relatively quick and inexpensive way of improving the survivability of U.S. strategic forces should the Soviet Union develop threatening antisubmarine capabilities, since SSBN patrols in the Indian Ocean would greatly magnify the area that would have to be searched by submarine detection systems.

   Deploying SSBNs to the Indian Ocean would not be without cost, however. A Poseidon submarine support facility (including a specialized tender) would have to be located somewhere in the region; otherwise the distance between the likely patrol area (the Arabian Sea) and the nearest existing facility (Guam) would be so great that the ratio between transit and on-station times would be cost-ineffective. Extensive topographic and hydrographic research would be necessary to ensure missile accuracy, and communication and navigation systems might have to be further developed. Moreover, once operational in 1979, Trident—the U.S. next-generation, longer-range submarine-launched missile—will provide alternatives to the Indian Ocean, such as patrols in the northern Pacific, which will compound the difficulty of locating strategic submarines. Finally, the U.S.–Soviet treaty limiting the deployment of

7. Arguments that the United States generally pays too much attention to verification problems in considering possible arms control agreements may be found in G. W. Rathjens, Abram Chayes, and J. P. Ruina, *Nuclear Arms Control Agreements: Process and Impact* (Washington, D.C.: Carnegie Endowment for World Peace, 1974).

antiballistic missile systems, signed in Moscow in 1972, undercuts much of the potential advantage of Indian Ocean submarine patrols.

7. *Cost avoidance.* A decision to maintain larger U.S. naval forces in the Indian Ocean could have an important effect on future U.S. Navy force levels and consequently on future navy budgets. If all other carrier deployments remained unchanged, three carriers would have to be added to the navy in order to maintain one continuously on station in the Indian Ocean.[8] And the number of escort vessels, support ships, and air wings maintained in the active navy would have to be adjusted accordingly. Acquiring these naval units would cost between $5 billion and $8 billion, depending upon the precise characteristics of the vessels and aircraft involved. Once these forces entered the fleet, annual navy operating costs would rise by about $800 million.[9]

Obviously, decisions about aircraft carrier force levels depend on many factors. And carrier deployments to the Indian Ocean could be supported, at least on an intermittent basis, by scaling down carrier deployments elsewhere. Nonetheless, the imposition of a requirement to maintain a carrier task force continuously in the Indian Ocean would greatly strengthen arguments for higher force levels, which might imply, at the outside, the costs mentioned above. Avoiding this growth in the defense budget is an additional reason to consider seriously the prospects for Indian Ocean naval disengagement.

8. So long as ships are not based within their deployment region, it generally requires three carriers in the inventory to maintain one on station. The backup carriers are necessary to account for maintenance and overhaul schedules, training needs, and the time delays required to outfit the ship and for it to transit between its home port and the operating region.

9. The minimum cost calculation assumes the addition of three carriers, ten escorts, two support ships, and two air wings of eighty aircraft each to the fleet.

CHAPTER SIX

CONCLUSIONS

There seems little likelihood in the near future that either the United States or the Soviet Union will agree to naval disengagement in any region of the world. Nor is it likely that they will initiate negotiations on the type of inventory limitation agreements discussed in this paper, regardless of their substantive merits and advantages to both sides. Nonetheless, although current prospects for naval arms control have to be rated poor, government officials and the public should continue to design and debate new ideas and proposals. It is with such a debate in mind that the arms control regimes mentioned in this paper have been outlined. The arguments bearing on the desirability and feasibility of these regimes are summarized below.

Limitation on Naval Inventories

One way to limit naval inventories is to set ceilings on measures of aggregate naval capability. Expenditures, operational manpower, and aggregate tonnage are suggested as possible indexes. This approach is not particularly promising, however. For one thing, some of the suggested limits would be difficult to negotiate because of existing disparities between the U.S. and Soviet Navies. More important, an agreement restricting only aggregate capabilities does not foreclose future military developments that might negate the superficial balance of naval power which the agreement specified.

The other type of agreement suggested in chapter 2 places separate limits on different types of ships and appears to offer greater potential benefits than overall restrictions. In my opinion, this approach deserves further investigation. There are three important considerations: the effect of the agreement on the balance of military power between the United States and the Soviet Union; its possible impact on U.S. foreign policy and on the risk of war between the superpowers; and finally, its fiscal implications.

Ceilings on the inventories of individual ship types (described on pages 24–28) would essentially freeze the naval balance between the United States and the Soviet Union, at least in a quantitative sense, as it is now projected for 1980. More ambitious proposals could be developed—that would either reduce existing force levels or add restraints on modernization rates to controls on inventories, but an agreement not to exceed projected ceilings appears to be the most realistic first step toward the limitation of naval arms. Such an agreement would maintain the vast superiority of the United States in sea-based airpower and the quantitative lead of the Soviet Union in attack and cruise missile submarines. It would guarantee parity between the two superpowers in the number and tonnage of oceangoing warships. The agreement would not, however, place any controls on other kinds of naval forces—land-based maritime aircraft, amphibious warfare, mine warfare, or support and auxiliary ships.

Any evaluation of this inventory limitation proposal should compare what is likely to occur beyond 1980 in the absence of agreement with what is likely to occur under the terms of the agreement. With regard to the naval balance, a freeze on force levels would seem, in general, to favor the Soviet Union. From the mid-1960s through the early 1970s, the USSR probably improved its naval capabilities relative to those of the United States. For various reasons, primarily relating to the psychological and economic costs of the war in Vietnam, the United States deferred a sharp response to this marked Soviet advance. The Soviet naval challenge is likely to provoke a more emphatic reaction in the future, however. Already, increases in U.S. shipbuilding programs since 1969 promise to reverse what had been a ten-year trend toward lower U.S. naval force levels. Assuming that U.S. naval building programs continue at present rates or expand, it is unlikely that the Soviet Union, with its much more modest economic and technological base, could avoid a reversal in the recent trend in relative naval capabilities. On the other hand, the balance of forces that is likely to exist in the 1980s is not one that would be markedly disadvantageous to the United States, and it is not clear that altering this balance could be translated into real advantages in terms of U.S. foreign policy or other national interests.

This type of inventory agreement probably would not have a direct impact on the risk of conflict between the superpowers; it is too general and nonconstraining for that. It could, however, help to reduce international political tension by complementing any agreements to limit strategic arms and to reduce forces in Europe. In fact, the impact on the political environment would be largely symbolic and psychological. It would indicate that the United States and the Soviet Union recognized the dangers implicit in naval rivalry, and that they were prepared to take steps to reduce these risks. Their agreement would be regarded as an important precedent that could lead to further, more exacting agreements in the future.

The agreement's impact on defense spending would be determined by three indirect effects. First, the cost of additional escalations in the naval arms race would not be incurred. Without such an agreement, it seems likely that the United States will maintain or even expand its present shipbuilding programs in response to recent changes in relative U.S.–USSR naval capabilities. In turn, the Soviet Union might feel compelled to step up its own building programs. Agreeing to freeze naval forces at projected 1980 levels would avoid these increased expenditures. Second, attainment of the agreement could, over the long run, strengthen arguments for unilateral reductions in spending for naval forces. If a superpower felt less threatened by its rival's naval armaments because the latter's intentions were more predictable, it might make selective slowdowns in modernization programs, not build up to the prescribed limits in ship categories controlled by the agreement, or make some reductions in uncontrolled categories of naval weapons. Third, as the first SALT agreements demonstrated, quite a different effect might obtain; some might argue that an arms control regime required accelerated modernization or an increase in the uncontrolled forces either to hedge against a breakdown of the agreement or to use as a bargaining tool in future more elaborate negotiations. Similarly, there would be strong pressures from the Navy and elsewhere to build up to the agreed limits, as evidence of U.S. resolve. The outcome would be influenced, in the end, by domestic economic and political pressures in each country. Much would depend on whether the freeze in force levels was viewed as a first step toward more ambitious naval arms control measures with more direct implications for defense spending, or as a final measure.

Limitations on Naval Deployments

There is little in the denuclearization proposal described in chapter 3 that merits serious attention. An agreement to prohibit warships carrying nuclear weapons in the Mediterranean or any other region would be difficult to verify and, more important, would be markedly disadvantageous to the United States.

An agreement to place broader limitations on U.S. and Soviet naval deployments to the Mediterranean or to the Indian Ocean—naval disengagement agreements—would balance advantages and disadvantages for both superpowers, and they thus deserve more careful examination than denuclearization. The illustrative agreement outlined in appendix B prohibits naval deployments by the signatories in the designated region (in the example, the Indian Ocean), except for intermittent cruises governed by restrictions on the purpose of the cruise, the size of the force, and the length of stay. It would be monitored by an international control commission, and it would also provide for the removal of naval support facilities from the littorals of the sea in question.

Naval Disengagement in the Mediterranean

Of the regions considered, the benefits of an agreement restricting naval deployments in the Mediterranean would be the most significant. They relate primarily to a reduced risk of conflict between the United States and the Soviet Union. Reaching such an agreement would be an important step toward a stable international situation; it would blunt the U.S.–Soviet confrontation at its most dangerous point. With no large standing vulnerable naval deployments in the Mediterranean, fears of preemptive attack would recede, and hence the need for quick decision and abrupt action. There should be fewer incidents or face-offs and less tension. Inadvertent superpower involvement in regional conflicts should be less likely; consequently, the local disputes themselves might be somewhat easier to control.

How Mediterranean disengagement would affect the military balance between the two superpowers is more ambiguous. While there is tactical advantage in not maintaining a large U.S. surface fleet in the relatively confined waters of the Mediterranean, the alternative in the event of a breakdown of the agreement—that is, the U.S. Navy fighting its way in through the narrow straits guarding the Sea—hinges on assumptions regarding timing, possible actions by littoral states, and other factors that are too numerous and complex to evaluate with any confidence.

In any case, a disengagement agreement covering the Mediterranean would probably provoke strong negative reactions on the part of important U.S. NATO allies, particularly Germany and Turkey, and it would greatly alarm Israel. Consequently, the benefits of Mediterranean disengagement with regard to U.S.–Soviet relations have to be weighed against a deterioration in U.S. relations with certain allies, which would be felt as soon as there was serious prospect of negotiation.

Finally, the situation in the Mediterranean is so unstable at present, particularly with regard to Arab-Israeli relations, and the conflicting interests of the superpowers are joined so sharply, that the political basis for a durable arms control regime seems to be lacking. Thus an agreement could probably not be negotiated at this time; if it were negotiated, it might well be overturned before its term had expired. These considerations argue for deferring any initiative leading to Mediterranean disengagement until the Middle East situation is closer to settlement. The intervening period can be used for consultation with U.S. allies to elicit their possible responses and to discuss with them possible advantages of U.S.–Soviet disengagement.

Naval Disengagement in the Indian Ocean

The benefits of disengagement in the Indian Ocean are not as great as in the Mediterranean; the risk of conflict between the United States and the USSR is far less. Yet it is precisely because the interests of the superpowers in the Indian Ocean are not as important as in the Mediterranean, and because they are in an earlier stage of naval competition, that the chances of reaching an Indian Ocean accord may be greater. Many of the arms control agreements reached by the United States and the Soviet Union have been in areas where there was only minor involvement, or the prospect of it, and in which the two superpowers, with the exception of special domestic interests, preferred to avoid an armaments race. Examples include not only the Treaty on the Limitation of Antiballistic Missile Systems (1972), but also the Antarctic Treaty (1961), the Treaty on the Prohibition of the Emplacement of Nuclear Weapons and Other Weapons of Mass Destruction on the Sea-Bed and in the Subsoil Thereof (1972), and the Convention on the Prohibition of the Development, Production, and Stockpiling of Bacteriological (Biological) and Toxic Weapons (1972). In each of these cases, the arms control regime permitted the superpowers to avoid expenditures on military systems that they felt were not important, but in which, without agreement, they might well have felt compelled to invest. Naval deployments in the Indian Ocean appear to have somewhat the same character.

There is widespread international interest in mitigating superpower competition in the Indian Ocean. In 1971, the United Nations General Assembly passed a resolution declaring the Indian Ocean to be a "zone of peace." The resolution, which was passed without opposition (but with more than sixty abstentions), called upon the great powers to eliminate their military presence from the region and urged the littoral states to establish procedures governing the passage of warships.[1] Since that time, the General Assembly has formed an ad hoc committee on the Indian Ocean, which has begun discussions of various aspects of the problems involved in implementing the resolution.[2] In July 1974, a panel of experts presented a report to the ad hoc committee describing the extent and composition of military deployments by external powers in the region.[3]

While the case for Indian Ocean naval disengagement is not one-sided, the long-term benefits of such an arrangement appear to outweigh its risks. The net advantage of maintaining standing U.S. naval forces in the region during peacetime, given the present status of the Soviet Navy, are not obvious. And the benefits of disengagement would be twofold: there would be less likelihood of a U.S.–Soviet confrontation in the Indian Ocean similar to the one in the Mediterranean; and the substantial costs implied by an increase in carrier requirements would be avoided.

It thus would seem to be in the U.S. interest to continue to seek agreement with the USSR. There is, however, a complication. Most of the contingencies in which the United States might want to use naval forces in the Indian Ocean are remote; but one—an armed intervention on the Persian Gulf to end a future oil embargo—is more immediate.

1. See the following UN documents: A/8584, December 14, 1971; A/PV. 2022, pp. 27–31; A/8492, October 1, 1971.

2. UN General Assembly, *Report of the Ad Hoc Committee on the Indian Ocean*, UN Doc. A/9029 (XXVIII), Supplement 29, 1973.

3. *Declaration of the Indian Ocean as a Zone of Peace: Statement Pursuant to Paragraphs 6 and 7 of General Assembly Resolution 3080 (XXVIII)*, UN Doc. A/AC. 159/1/Rev 1, July 11, 1974. Interestingly, the experts at first issued a more detailed report which was withdrawn following protest by all the external powers (see UN Doc. A/AC. 159/1, May 3, 1974).

The President, the secretary of state, and the secretary of defense have all raised the prospect of intervention as a measure of last resort should a future embargo cause a desperate economic situation in the West.[4] The implicit threat contained in these statements has been reinforced by naval maneuvers and diplomatic activity. The administration's purpose in posing this threat is not obvious, but it may be designed to restore momentum to the Arab-Israeli peace negotiations.[5]

A serious American initiative for superpower naval disengagement in the Indian Ocean unfortunately would undercut the threat of military intervention and thereby undermine the policy the threat is meant to support. Until the present differences between oil-producing and oil-consuming states are alleviated somewhat or the Arab-Israeli talks take a more optimistic turn, therefore, it might be prudent to regard superpower naval disengagement in the Indian Ocean more as a desirable objective than as an immediate prospect.

There is also always the possibility that future events will make it advisable for the United States to revive the threat of intervention in this area. But a naval deployment limitation agreement—unlike controls on naval inventories—need not have an enduring effect on the nation's military capabilities. Should a disengagement agreement be attained, but then political developments in the area proceed adversely, the agreement could be abrogated and a U.S. naval presence reestablished following any mandatory delay built into the agreement.

In the meantime, possible ways of implementing an Indian Ocean naval disengagement agreement, such as the one discussed in this paper, should be investigated further. Soviet interest in this prospect, as well as in the two other measures of naval arms control that I suggest show promise (limitations on certain kinds of ships in the two superpowers' inventories and disengagement in the Mediterranean), might also be probed through unofficial channels. Although the chances for limiting the superpowers' navies seem poor at present, one should not lose sight of the benefits to be derived from measures to control this important area of U.S.–Soviet competition.

4. See reports of Gerald R. Ford in *New York Times*, January 22, 1975; and Henry M. Kissinger in "Kissinger on Oil, Food, and Trade," *Business Week*, January 13, 1975, p. 69; and the report of the news conference with Secretary of Defense James R. Schlesinger on January 14, 1975.

5. I discuss this possibility in an article, "Force and Diplomacy," *Washington Post*, February 7, 1975.

THE U.S. AND SOVIET GENERAL PURPOSE NAVIES: AN OVERVIEW

No nation will agree to limit naval armaments unless it can reasonably predict the size and composition of rival navies in the years ahead. That is one purpose of this appendix—to forecast what the conventional naval forces of the United States and the Soviet Union will look like in the year 1980. It furnishes a tangible basis for the analyses in chapter 2 of possible naval inventory limitation agreements.

In addition, this appendix provides background for the discussion in chapters 4 and 5 of possible disengagement in the Mediterranean and Indian Ocean by describing U.S. and Soviet naval operations in the regions.

The American Navy

At the end of fiscal 1975, the U.S. Navy will consist of about 500 ships that will together displace close to 6 million tons. There will be about 540,000 men and women in naval uniform, and another 200,000 in Marine dress. And the Navy's budget for the year will total about $28 billion.

The most important element in the U.S. Navy is still the aircraft carrier. The carrier building program and carrier force levels are therefore the most important factors in determining the overall size of the Navy, as well as its budget.

Aircraft Carriers and Amphibious Warfare Forces

These forces in 1974 and 1980 are compared in Table A-1. Defense officials have indicated that the United States will maintain a force of

Table A-1. U.S. Aircraft Carrier and Amphibious Warfare Forces, 1974 and 1980

Type of vessel and designation	Class	Number of ships	
		1974	*1980*
Full-size aircraft carriers			
CVN	Nimitz (nuclear-powered)	0	2
CVN	Enterprise (nuclear-powered)	1	1
CV	Forrestal and Kitty Hawk	8	8
CVA	Midway	3	1
CVA	Hancock	2	0
Helicopter carriers			
LHA	Tarawa	0	5
LPH	Iwo Jima	7	7
Command ships			
LCC	Blue Ridge	2	2
AGF	LaSalle	1	1
Cargo ships			
LKA	Charleston	5	5
LKA	Tulare	1	0
Transports			
LPA	Paul Revere	2	1
LPD	Austin	12	12
LPD	Raleigh	2	0
Landing ships			
LSD	Anchorage	5	5
LSD	Thomaston	8	0
LST	Newport	20	20

Sources: Author's estimates based on information supplied by Chief of Naval Operations Admiral J. L. Holloway to Representative Les Aspin, July 3, 1974; John E. Moore (ed.), *Jane's Fighting Ships, 1973/1974* (Sampson Low, 1973). There are the following assumptions: (1) the United States can maintain only twelve full-size carriers in 1980 because of obsolescence; (2) amphibious warfare ships have a commissioned life of twenty years; and (3) no new amphibious warfare ships will be authorized in the next several years.

twelve full-size aircraft carriers in the 1980s: four nuclear-powered vessels and eight with conventional power of the *Forrestal* and *Kitty Hawk* classes, seven of which were built in the 1950s. The last carrier of World War II construction—the *Midway*—will be retired as the third *Nimitz*-class nuclear-powered ship—the *Vinson*—enters service around 1982. The fully modernized 1980s force will displace about 1 million tons at full load.

All told, this force will carry approximately 1,100 aircraft. The mix of aircraft types will vary by ship, but air wings will consist primarily of F-14 fighters for defensive missions, A-7s for ground and surface-ship attack, and S-3s for antisubmarine warfare. As in the present force, there will be some F-4s and A-6s, as well as various reconnaissance, early warning, and electronic warfare aircraft. In general, air wings will gain some defensive capability—the addition of F-14s, equipped with Phoenix missiles, and S-3s—at the expense of ground-attack capability.

The U.S. Navy planned to have a new kind of carrier in its inventory around 1980—the sea control ship. This vessel, with a displacement of about 14,000 tons, would have carried vertical or short takeoff and landing aircraft (V/STOL) and helicopters. It was to be used primarily for the defense of merchant shipping, replenishment ships, and amphibious task forces against enemy submarines and surface ships. It would also be able to project air power ashore in certain situations if the aircraft on board were suitably configured. The Congress denied funds for this program in fiscal 1975, however, and instructed the Navy to design a larger and more capable ship for this mission. The new class will not enter the Navy's active inventory until after 1980.

The U.S. force of amphibious warfare ships, which was extensively modernized in the 1960s, will remain virtually intact over the next seven years. The major exception will be the addition of the five *Tarawa*-class amphibious assault ships now under construction. These 40,000-ton vessels will carry thirty helicopters, landing craft, and the men and equipment (including armor) for a reinforced Marine battalion. Seven smaller helicopter assault ships will also remain in the force. There will be some minor reductions in landing and cargo ships, and in transports, as the remaining pre-1960-vintage vessels are retired.

Surface Warships

U.S. surface combatant force levels are likely to increase by about 13 percent between 1974 and 1980. The composition and capabilities of the force will also change markedly. The increase in number of surface combatants—from 211 in 1974 to 239 in 1980—will reverse the trend toward lower force levels evident in the past six years. Other significant retirements include fifty-five destroyers first built in the 1940s but subsequently modernized, and four older cruisers. Major additions to the surface combatant force could consist of six nuclear-powered cruisers of the *Virginia* and *California* classes, thirty *Spruance*-class destroyers, twenty-four of a planned fifty-ship fleet of guided missile frigates, and thirty ships of a new type—a missile-equipped hydrofoil patrol vessel. Force levels are summarized in Table A-2.

Table A-2. U.S. Surface Combatant Forces, 1974 and 1980

Type of vessel and designation	*Class*	*Number of ships*	
		1974	*1980*
Cruisers			
CGN	Long Beach (nuclear-powered)	1	1
CA	Salem	1	0
CG	Albany	3	0
CGN	Virginia (nuclear-powered)	0	4[a]
CGN	California (nuclear-powered)	1	2
CGN	Truxtun (nuclear-powered)	1	1
CGN	Bainbridge (nuclear-powered)	1	1
CG	Belknap	9	9
CG	Leahy	9	9
Destroyers			
DD	Spruance	0	30
DDG	Adams	23	23
DDG	Sherman	14	14
DDG	Decatur	4	4
DG	Farragut	8	10
DD	Mitscher	2	0
DD	Fram I and II	55	0
Frigates			
FFG	Guided missile frigate	0	24
FF	Knox	44	46
FFG	Brooke	6	6
FF	Garcia	10	10
FF	Bronstein	2	2
FF	Jones	2	0
Patrol combatants[b]			
PG	Asheville and Tacoma	15	10
PHM	Pegasus	0	30
SES	Surface effect ship	0	3

Sources: Same as Table A-1. There are the following assumptions: the effective lifetime for cruisers is thirty years; for destroyers, twenty-five years; and for smaller vessels, twenty years.

a. It is assumed that one new nuclear-powered cruiser is authorized each year, pointing to a total force of sixteen.

b. There are also about thirty oceangoing vessels with some combat capabilities assigned to the U.S. Coast Guard.

Qualitatively, the surface combatant force will be much improved. In 1980, the average age of the force will be less than ten years, compared to the present average age of slightly above fourteen years. There will be nine, rather than four, nuclear-powered vessels. And the number of ships equipped with surface-to-air missile systems will increase by almost 60 percent; those with antisubmarine rocket systems by one-fourth; and those with helicopter support facilities by about one-half.

For the first time, a significant number of U.S. naval vessels will be outfitted with surface-to-surface missiles—maybe 100 by 1980. In terms of individual vessel size[1] the force will decrease slightly: mean tonnage dropping from 4,400 tons to 4,300 tons.[2] Most of the new ships will be of relatively small size (as U.S. Navy ships run) including the guided missile frigate at 3,400 tons, and the hydrofoil patrol vessel at 200 tons. The only large ships to be added are the nuclear-powered cruisers—about 10,000 tons apiece—and the *Spruance*-class destroyers, at about 7,000 tons.

Attack Submarines

The 1980s will witness a major expansion in the capabilities of the U.S. force of attack submarines, as the increase in submarine construction initiated in the late 1960s begins to pay off. Thirteen new nuclear-powered submarines will be commissioned between 1974 and 1980, including the remaining three of the *Sturgeon* class, nine of the new *Los Angeles* class, and an experimental submarine, the *Lipscomb*. Retirements, with the possible exception of one or two early nuclear boats (for example, the *Nautilus*) will be restricted to diesel-powered submarines, and the force should be exclusively nuclear-propelled by 1980. The bulk of the force will be composed of the *Sturgeon* and *Los Angeles* classes. These vessels, both relatively large but quiet boats, are primarily designed and equipped to counter other submarines. The newer *Los Angeles* class is considerably larger than its predecessors. U.S. submarine force levels are summarized in Table A-3.

Other Elements

Any assessment of naval capabilities has to include other elements besides the number and characteristics of the major combatant vessels described above. There are land-based aircraft. Aside from the possible contribution of U.S. Air Force aircraft—much discussed but seldom acted upon—the only important element in this connection is the land-based antisubmarine patrol aircraft. There are twenty-four such squadrons in the active force, consisting of P-3 *Orion* aircraft. The Navy has

1. Vessel size reflects, although certainly not in a rigorous manner, qualitative characteristics, such as endurance, reload capacity, crew habitability, and the like. More efficient ship design can sometimes compensate for smaller vessel size.
2. All tonnages represent full-load displacement.

Table A-3. U.S. Submarine Fleets, 1974 and 1980

	Number of submarines	
Type and class	*1974*	*1980*
Strategic submarines	**41**	**43**
Trident	0	2
Lafayette	31	31
Ethan Allen	5	5
George Washington	5	5
Attack submarines	**71**	**71**
Nuclear-powered		
Los Angeles[a]	0	9
Sturgeon	34	37
Permit	13	13
Skipjack	5	5
Skate	4	4
Other	3	3
Total, nuclear-powered	59	71
Diesel-powered		
Various classes	12	0
Total	**112**	**114**

Sources: Same as Table A-1.
a. Delivery schedule is given in *Fiscal Year 1975 Authorization for Military Procurement, Research and Development, and Active Duty, Selected Reserve and Civilian Personnel Strengths*, Hearings before the Senate Committee on Armed Services, 93 Cong. 2 sess. (1974), pt. 3, p. 1205.

been replacing older versions of this plane with ones that have better detection equipment at the rate of twelve per year. There are also twelve squadrons of antisubmarine aircraft in the naval reserve forces that are being supplied with the older P-3 aircraft as they are being replaced in the active force with the newer models.

Then there are the support fleets—the ships that are to replenish, maintain, and repair combatant vessels. The United States has invested considerable funds in these forces in the past and their capabilities are generally recognized. Particularly important is the fleet of about sixty replenishment ships: oil tankers and ammunition ships that fuel and supply combatant vessels on the high seas and that enable the United States to maintain surface forces at sea for protracted periods of time under hostile conditions. In fiscal 1975, the United States initiated a major shipbuilding program to modernize these support ships.

Another element that should be considered is the overseas infrastructure—communications sites, ordnance and fuel depots, repair yards, and the like in regions far from the home country—that makes it easier to maintain naval forces on the high seas for long periods. Between the Second World War and the late 1950s, the United States set up an extensive network of military bases overseas. Key naval facilities were located in the Caribbean, Iceland, the United Kingdom, Spain, the Azores, Italy, Greece, Morocco, Bahrain, Australia, Japan, the Philippines, various Pacific islands, and elsewhere. While there has been a general tendency to cut back on this overseas presence in more recent years, one important exception has been the establishment of overseas home ports for naval ships. Previously almost all ships of the Sixth Fleet (deployed in the Mediterranean) and the Seventh Fleet (deployed in the Western Pacific) were based in the United States and rotated to their deployment areas for periods of about six to nine months. Now, considerations of reduced force levels and personnel retention problems have led to more frequent use of foreign harbors as home ports.[3]

The U.S. Military Presence in the Mediterranean and Indian Ocean

There were approximately 66,000 U.S. military personnel in and along the littorals of both the Mediterranean and the Indian Ocean at the end of 1974. Their distribution is shown in Table A-4.

In terms of manpower (and cost) and, more important, in terms of political saliency, the most important component is the Sixth Fleet, which has been deployed to the Mediterranean for twenty-five years. In many respects this fleet symbolizes American commitment to the region. It usually has a complement of between forty and forty-five ships, including the following: the flagship, a cruiser; two aircraft carrier task forces, each with a tactical air wing (eighty-five or ninety aircraft) and about six escort ships; an amphibious assault task group of six vessels with a Marine battalion landing team of 1,800 men and their equipment on board; several submarines; miscellaneous escort ships not attached to the carrier or amphibious task group; and various logistical support and other auxiliary vessels.

The United States maintains only a small standing naval force in the

---

3. Under the old system ships would make port calls for replenishment and crew shore leave during their rotations overseas. Now, using foreign harbors as home ports, however, crews' families live overseas and replenishment, storage, and some repair facilities are maintained under U.S. control.

Table A-4. U.S. Military Personnel in the Mediterranean and Indian Ocean, 1973

Region	Number
Afloat with Sixth Fleet in the Mediterranean	29,000
Italy	12,000
Spain	9,000
Turkey	7,000
Greece	4,000
British Indian Ocean territory	1,000
Morocco	1,000
Bahrain, Iran, and elsewhere	3,000
Total	66,000

Sources: *Report on Authorizing Appropriations for Fiscal Year 1975 for Military Procurement, Research and Development, and Active Duty, Selected Reserve and Civilian Personnel Strengths, and Other Purposes,* S. Rept. 93-884, 93 Cong. 2 sess. (1974), insert facing p. 134; *U.S. News and World Report* (December 30, 1974).

Indian Ocean. This squadron, known as the Middle East Force, consists of a command ship—*LaSalle*—and two destroyers on temporary detachment from the Atlantic fleet.

In 1973, during the Arab-Israeli October war, the United States began to deploy task forces to the Indian Ocean, on an intermittent basis, to strengthen its military presence. These task forces, which are dispatched from the Seventh Fleet in the Pacific, have consisted of either an aircraft carrier with its accompanying escorts and support ships, or a smaller group consisting of a cruiser and several escorts. In the fifteen months following the October 1973 war, the augmented force has been present in the Indian Ocean about 70 percent of the time.

The United States maintains no ground forces in the Mediterranean or Indian Ocean regions except for some support and auxiliary units in Italy and the Marine battalion with the Sixth Fleet. There are land-based tactical air forces in southern Europe, however. Three to six of the twenty-one U.S. Air Force tactical air squadrons in Europe are generally deployed to Italy, Turkey, or Spain. These provide a quick-reaction capability for Mediterranean contingencies. There also are two Navy land-based antisubmarine aircraft squadrons deployed in the Mediterranean area.

At times of crisis, these forces can be reinforced relatively quickly: the Sixth Fleet by units from the Second Fleet deployed in the Atlantic; the Indian Ocean squadron from the Seventh Fleet in the Western Pacific. Additional land-based tactical air forces can be flown into the Middle East from bases in Germany and England. If necessary, U.S.

ground troops can also be deployed from Germany or from the strategic reserve based in the United States.

The shorebased infrastructure supporting U.S. naval deployments in the Mediterranean and Indian Ocean is widely dispersed. The home port of the Sixth Fleet's flagship is Gaeta, Italy; some submarines and support ships are also based in Italy. The Navy had planned to use Greece as a home port for a carrier task force, but the idea will probably be dropped because of the sharp change in Greek policy. Other ships of the Sixth Fleet are based in the United States and assigned to the Mediterranean for tours of about six months. In addition to home ports, the Sixth Fleet makes use of various facilities, such as ordnance depots and communications stations, in Morocco, Spain, Italy, Greece, and Turkey.

The home port of the flagship of the Middle East Force is Bahrain. In fall 1973, the sheikh of Bahrain asked the United States to leave within one year, but in January 1975 the status of negotiations on this question was still unclear. Other U.S. facilities along the Indian Ocean include communications sites in Australia, Diego Garcia, and Ethiopia (where facilities are being phased out). The Navy has requested authorization from Congress to expand its facilities on Diego Garcia. If approved, it seems likely that long-range reconnaissance and antisubmarine warfare aircraft will be based there. The harbor will also be enlarged to accommodate a carrier, and petroleum storage and other facilities will be constructed.

The Soviet Navy

Within the past ten years the Soviet Union has begun to expand the role of its Navy, moving from a strictly defensive posture with a force reserved for wartime contingencies to a more flexible one with a force that is useful in a variety of peacetime missions. To achieve this about face, however, the Soviet Navy will have to undergo considerable change. Some of the weaknesses and strengths of the present and projected 1980 Soviet Navy are described below.

Submarines

Soviet submarine force levels have been sharply declining in recent years as boats constructed before the 1960s are retired and not replaced on a one-for-one basis. In mid-1974, the Soviet fleet of attack and cruise missile submarines numbered about 252, including 74 nuclear-powered vessels—a big reduction from a total of nearly 500 in the late fifties. The decline will continue through this decade and into the 1980s as the remaining diesel-powered submarines, which were built in very large numbers during the 1950s, are retired. Assuming submarine construction continues at the rates evident since 1968, the 1980 force will number approximately 196 (including 120 nuclear-powered boats).[4] The composition of the present and the projected 1980 Soviet submarine forces is shown in Table A-5.

The more modern submarines are far more capable than their predecessors, however, and the projected submarine fleet will continue to present a considerable challenge to Western maritime forces. The 1980 force will probably have 60 percent more nuclear-powered submarines (120) than the 1974 one (75). It also will include a 40 percent increase in the number of nuclear submarines equipped with cruise missiles (40 in 1974, 56 in 1980); but because some diesel-powered submarines will be retired, the total number of cruise missile launchers in the force will increase by only about 20 percent. The latest model submarine-launched cruise missile, the SS-N-7 (which is of short range, but which can be launched underwater and needs no external target information), is considered a far more effective weapon than its predecessors.

Additionally, the Soviet submarines that made their first appearance in the late 1960s (the *Charley, Papa, Alpha,* and *Victor* classes), although still qualitatively inferior to modern U.S. submarines except in underwater speed, are generally considered to indicate considerable technological advances. These improvements include noise level (and therefore survivability), propulsion systems, and on-board detection systems. Moreover, if past performance is any guide, even newer and more capable classes of cruise missile and torpedo attack submarines should make their appearance before the end of the decade.

Surface Warships

The Soviet force of surface combatants is shown in Table A-6. There were approximately 575 combatant vessels displacing more than 200 tons in the USSR's active inventory in mid-year 1974.[5] About 60 per-

4. This figure and the totals given for 1958 and 1974 do not include strategic submarines.
5. The 200-ton limit excludes patrol boats and other small craft.

Table A-5. Soviet Submarine Fleets, 1974 and 1980

	Number of submarines			
	1974		1980	
Type and class	Nuclear-powered	Diesel-powered	Nuclear-powered	Diesel-powered
Strategic	**45**	**22**	**62**	**12**
Delta	3		28	
Yankee	33		34	
Hotel	9		0	
Gulf		18		12
Zulu		4		0
Nonstrategic	**74**	**178**	**120**	**76**
Cruise missile				
Charley/Papa/Follow-on class[a]	13		29	
Echo II	27		27	
Juliet		16		16
Whiskey (conversions)[b]		9		0
Cruise missile, total	40	25	56	16
Attack				
Alpha/Victor/Follow-on class[a]	19		42	
Echo I/Hotel	3		12	
November	13		10	
Foxtrot		56		50
Zulu		25		0
Whiskey		36		0
Romeo		12		0
Bravo		4		10
Quebec		20		0
Attack, total	35	153	64	60
Total	**120**	**200**	**182**	**88**

Sources: Same as Table A-1. See also Robert P. Berman, "Soviet Naval Strength and Deployment," and Michael K. MccGwire, "Current Soviet Warship Construction and Naval Weapons Development," in Michael K. MccGwire, Kenneth Boothe, and John McDonnell (eds.), *Soviety Naval Policy: Objectives and Constraints* (Praeger, 1975), pp. 419–23 and 424–51, respectively. There are the following assumptions: (1) No new strategic ballistic missile submarines (SSBNs) will appear before 1980; the *Delta* class will be the primary SSBN and no existing *Yankee* will be converted to the *Delta* configuration; all *Hotel*-class submarines will be converted to attack submarines so as to maximize the number of sea-based missiles within restrictions of the strategic arms limitation agreements. (2) All diesel-powered submarines are to be retired at twenty years of age. (3) All *Hotel* and *Echo I* submarines are to be converted to torpedo attack submarines (they both have essentially the *November*-class hull design and propulsion system).
  a. Past experience indicates that new classes of cruise missile and attack submarines will appear before 1980.
  b. Between 1958 and 1963 a number of *Whiskey*-class attack submarines were modified to accommodate cruise missiles.

cent of this total—343 ships—consisted of smaller vessels, primarily corvettes and patrol vessels, used for the defense of coastal waters. The remainder were 2 antisubmarine helicopter carriers, 29 cruisers, 80 destroyers, and 121 frigates. It is the latter types of vessels that are of

Table A-6. Soviet Warships, 1974 and 1980

	Number of ships	
Type and class	*1974*	*1980*
Carriers for vertical and short takeoff and landing aircraft and helicopters		
Kiev	0	3
Moskva	2	2
Cruisers		
Kara/Follow-on class[a]	1	9
Kresta II	5	8
Kresta I	4	4
Kynda	4	4
Sverdlov[b]	12	8
Chapaev	2	0
Kirov	1	0
Destroyers		
Krivak/Follow-on class[a]	5	29
Kashin	19	19
Kanin	6	8
Krupny	1	0
Kotlin (SAM-equipped)	8	8
Kildin	2	2
Kotlin	18	18
Skory	20	0
Tallin	1	0
Frigates		
Grisha/Follow-on class[a]	13	26
Kola	5	0
Riga	35	0
Mirka	25	25
Petya	43	43
Other types (displacing at least 200 tons at full load)		
Nanuchka	8	20
Osa/Follow-on class[a]	120	120
Poti/Kronstadt/So-1/Stenka/Follow-on class[a]	215	185

Sources: Same as Table A-5.
a. Past experience indicates that new classes of cruisers, destroyers, frigates, and other types displacing at least 200 tons will appear before 1980.
b. It is assumed that these vessels, built between 1951 and 1956, will be modernized with new air defense, communications, and electronic warfare equipment. Two vessels have already been modified.

greatest interest in evaluating Soviet naval capabilities vis-à-vis those of the United States—or in the context of naval arms control.

The composition of the Soviet surface fleet will change substantially over the next six years as vessels built during the 1950s are replaced with more modern units. As in the case of the Soviet submarine fleet, there will be a decrease in force levels. The decline will not be nearly so steep for warships, however, probably not exceeding 10 percent. Newer units entering the fleet are also considerably more capable than their predecessors. Each new class entering the force—*Kara*-class cruisers, *Krivak*-class destroyers, and *Grisha*-class frigates—have been admired in the West, particularly in regard to design, propulsion system, and on-board weapons capability.

Generally, the units entering the force are larger than their older counterparts. The mean full-load displacement of active ships of escort size and larger will rise by about 20 percent over the next six years. This is largely due to the addition of three aircraft carriers (about 40,000 tons each) and a moderate shift to cruisers and larger destroyers at the expense of escorts. It probably indicates greater performance capability in range, endurance, reload capacity, crew habitability, and space for command staffs and communications gear.

The 1980 force will be better prepared for air defense. The number of ships equipped with surface-to-air missiles (SAMs) is likely to double, and the number of SAM rails available to the fleet will increase by about 70 percent. The 1980 force also will contain more ships with surface-to-surface missiles (SSMs). Not counting missile boats (*Komar, Osa,* and *Nanuchka* classes) used in coastal and other protected waters, there were 22 ships with SSMs in the 1974 force, carrying a total of 122 tubes. In 1980, the number of ships with SSMs should more than double to 59; they will sport more than 300 tubes. There is also considerable improvement in the qualitative features of these missiles, and in Soviet antisubmarine weapons, detection systems, and electronic warfare equipment. The Soviets have not, however, begun construction of nuclear-powered surface warships.

By far the most marked change in the 1980 force will be the introduction of small aircraft carriers. The USSR's lack of sea-based air power has long been one of the major deficiencies in its Navy, but present construction of at least two *Kiev*-class carriers indicates that they are attempting to correct this situation. The new carriers will be small by U.S. standards (40,000 tons versus 90,000 tons for the new U.S. *Nimitz* class). Also, they do not seem to be equipped with catapults or arresting gear, which would be necessary if high-performance jet aircraft were to be deployed on the ships. Consequently, the new vessels will be restricted to helicopters and vertical or short takeoff and landing aircraft. The Soviet Union, within the past several years, has tested such aircraft on its even smaller *Moskva*-class carriers.

While the physical characteristics of the new ships are relatively discernible, their mission remains enigmatic. Speculation in the West tends to focus on antisubmarine warfare, reconnaissance, or air defense of other surface units. The limited lift capacity of the V/STOL aircraft, which the Soviets so far have demonstrated publicly, would seem to preclude a projection role, such as that assigned to U.S. carriers. My forecast of three *Kiev* carriers in 1980 assumes that the Soviets continue to devote only one building way to this size of warship, as they have done until 1975.

Other Elements

There are four other elements in the Soviet Navy to consider when comparing its relative strengths and weaknesses with the U.S. Navy: its mine warfare capability and the naval air arm, which are comparatively strong, and its amphibious assault and support forces, which are comparatively weak.

MINE WARFARE CAPABILITIES. The Soviet Navy traditionally has placed considerable emphasis on mine warfare, much more so than is typically the case in Western navies. Although mines are most useful in defense—to protect coastal areas and ports from opposing forces—they can sometimes play a more provocative role. For example, relative mine warfare capabilities could contribute to the success or failure of sea-based interventionary expeditions. Or, mines could be used to exert pressure on an adversary by closing straits important to its economy, such as the entrance to the Persian Gulf.

At present the USSR maintains approximately 200 oceangoing mine-sweepers. This number will decline as a new class—the *Natya*—which first made its appearance in 1971, replaces older vessels. Nonetheless, the force is likely to remain large. There are also about 100 coastal minesweepers in the Soviet active inventory and a new class of this type has been identified.

Although the Soviet Union no longer deems it necessary to include minelaying as a capability on all its surface warships, it is still an important consideration. *Badger* medium-range aircraft, of which there are almost 300 in the Soviet naval air arm, can probably carry about twenty mines apiece.[6] Many submarines can also be used for minelaying.

---

6. This figure assumes they are not also carrying air-to-surface missiles. *Badgers* without ASMs are reported to carry 9 tons of ordnance internally; see John

Diesel-powered *Zulu*-class submarines are said to be able to carry about 40 mines apiece; *Foxtrot*-class submarines are likely to have similar capabilities. Present-day Soviet nuclear submarines are believed to be able to carry up to 64 mines apiece.[7]

THE NAVAL AIR ARM. There are approximately 1,200 aircraft of all types deployed with the Soviet naval air arm. Aside from antisubmarine helicopters based on the two *Moskva*-class carriers and on newer cruisers, however, these units are land-based. This situation could change (as noted above) by the addition of V/STOL aircraft once the *Kiev* becomes operational. The largest part of the air arm is the strike force. *Badgers*, carrying air-to-surface missiles, and longer-range *Bears*, for reconnaissance, make up the bulk of this force. There has been some speculation that the new Soviet medium-range bomber—the *Backfire* —will replace the *Badger*. Even without this modernization, however, the force of strike aircraft would pose a substantial threat to surface forces deployed within range of their home bases. If the Soviets could secure air bases overseas, this threat would be much greater.

The Soviet Navy has been rather slow to deploy modern land-based antisubmarine patrol aircraft. They do have one—the *May*—that has the capability, but little is known about the quality of its detection, localization, and weapons subsystems. And in any case, only thirty *May* aircraft are reported to have been deployed. There is also an antisubmarine amphibian aircraft of older design.

AMPHIBIOUS ASSAULT FORCES. Soviet sea-based interventionary capabilities are modest. The Soviet naval infantry consists of about 17,000 men. The newest and largest ship in the Soviet amphibious force—the *Alligator* class—resembles a landing ship (tank), one of the smaller U.S. vessels used for such purposes. There are no commando or helicopter assault ships in the Soviet Navy, and, in early 1975 at least, the Soviets were unable to supply sea-based air cover to project their power ashore. While there are about 100 vessels in the Soviet amphibious force (excluding landing craft), it is doubtful if their aggregate full-load displacement exceeds 150,000 tons. These figures can be compared to

---

W. R. Taylor and Gordon Swanborough, *Military Aircraft of the World* (Charles Scribner's Sons, 1971), p. 133.

7. John E. Moore (ed.), *Jane's Fighting Ships, 1973/1974* (Sampson Low, 1973), p. 544; Lieutenant Commander Robert D. Wells, "The Soviet Submarine Force," in *U.S. Naval Institute Proceedings*, vol. 97 (August 1971), pp. 63–79. Some of this mine capacity would be used, however, to carry torpedoes for self-defense.

the 200,000 Marines maintained by the United States and the more than 870,000 tons displaced by the sixty-three amphibious assault ships in the U.S. active inventory in 1974.

SUPPORT FORCES. The Soviet Navy's ability to maintain combatant forces under hostile conditions for protracted periods is seriously impaired by the inadequacies of its support forces. There are indications, however, that the Soviets are attempting to correct these deficiencies.

The role of support ships has been seriously underemphasized. Most of the new construction vessels of this type tend to emphasize the support of submarines and their missiles. Generally, the Soviet surface navy has had to make do with civilian merchant ships and tankers converted for military use. A new type of ship was identified under construction at Leningrad in 1971, however, which, according to *Jane's*, "is the first Soviet Navy purpose[ly] built underway fleet replenishment ship for the supply of both liquids and solids, indicating a growing awareness of the need for afloat support for a widely dispersed fleet."[8] This new ship, the *Boris Chilikin,* displaces about 20,000 tons. A smaller version, displacing about 7,500 tons, is being constructed in Finland. The Soviet Navy, according to Admiral Zumwalt, also has begun in recent years to practice side-by-side replenishment techniques —a much more efficient method of resupply than the bow-to-stern method traditionally practiced by Soviet naval vessels.[9]

Soviet Naval Activity in the Mediterranean and Indian Ocean

The introduction of Soviet naval forces into the Mediterranean did not begin on a sustained basis until the mid-1960s and the Soviet presence there did not grow significantly until after the 1967 Arab-Israeli war. The size of the Soviet Mediterranean fleet has more than doubled since that time. Soviet warships began to deploy to the Indian Ocean in 1968. Their presence there was enlarged substantially since then. Table A-7 indicates the growing number of ship-operating days spent in these two regions between 1965 and 1974.

This is not a very good measure of naval activity, however, because ship-operating days count every ship equally. Thus support ships, such as oilers, are counted as well as major combatants. When only combatant

8. *Jane's Fighting Ships, 1973/1974,* p. 582.
9. Letter from Admiral E. R. Zumwalt, Jr., to Senator William Proxmire, June 8, 1972; reprinted in *Congressional Record,* June 12, 1972, pp. 9193–95.

Table A-7. Growth of the Soviet Naval Presence in the Middle East, by Number of Ship-Operating Days, 1965–74

Year	Mediterranean[a]	Indian Ocean[b]
1965	4,000	c
1966	4,500	c
1967	8,500	c
1968	12,000	1,200
1969	14,000	4,000
1970	17,500	5,000
1971	19,000	4,000
1972	18,000	8,800[d]
1973	20,000	9,000[d]
1974	20,000	10,600[d]

Sources: Indian Ocean, 1965–73: *Military Procurement Supplemental—Fiscal Year 1974*, Hearings before the Senate Armed Services Committee, 93 Cong. 2 sess. (1974), p. 52; Mediterranean, 1965–74, and Indian Ocean, 1974: U.S. Navy sources.
a. Figures rounded to nearest 500.
b. Figures rounded to nearest 200.
c. Figures less than 100.
d. The large increase in 1972–74 is mainly the result of port-clearing operations in Bangladesh.

vessels are considered both the magnitude of the Soviet presence and its rate of growth appear much less. For the Indian Ocean, support and auxiliary vessels account for about 60 percent of the totals. Operations by minesweepers clearing the ports of Bangladesh account for another 10 percent. While total Soviet ship-operating days in the Indian Ocean increased by 125 percent between 1971 and 1973, those for combatants (exclusive of those in Bangladesh) increased by only 68 percent.[10]

The Soviet Mediterranean fleet typically consists of close to fifty vessels, less than half of which are warships and submarines. The force usually includes two cruisers, five to eight destroyers or other escorts, and about nine submarines. One of the two Soviet helicopter carriers (which are used for antisubmarine warfare) is seen frequently in the Mediterranean as well. Reinforcement of the force in time of crisis is always possible. For example, between October 5 and October 31, 1973, the Soviet Mediterranean fleet increased from a force of 16 surface combatants and 27 auxiliary vessels, to 29 surface combatants and 46 auxiliaries.[11] Reinforcement of the Soviet fleet during time of

10. Estimates derived from data appearing in *Military Procurement Supplemental—Fiscal Year 1974*, Hearings before the Senate Armed Services Committee, 93 Cong. 2 sess. (1974), p. 52.
11. *Fiscal Year 1975 Authorization for Military Procurement, Research and Development, and Active Duty, Selected Reserve and Civilian Personnel Strengths*, Hearings before the Senate Committee on Armed Services, 93 Cong. 2 sess. (1974), pt. 2, p. 533. Data for submarines were deleted from the testimony.

war would be more difficult, however, because U.S. allies control both entrances to the Mediterranean. Other Soviet forces that could affect the outcome of a conflict in the Mediterranean include, most importantly, strike aircraft based near the Black Sea. These planes would pose a considerable threat to U.S. surface naval forces operating within their effective combat range.

Except for the brief introduction of air units into Egypt in 1969 and 1970, the Soviet land-based presence in the Middle East has been negligible. Similarly, the Soviet Navy makes little use of shore facilities for the support of their naval forces. Along the Mediterranean, some Soviet facilities are located in Syria. In the Indian Ocean, the USSR maintains a communications site and a barracks ship and tenders in Somalia. Otherwise, the Soviet Navy relies on repairing and replenishing its ships while they are at anchor in sheltered areas, or the use of various ports on a commercial basis. This results, among other things, in Soviet ships spending a good deal of their sea time at anchor and inactive. However, there are recurring reports that the USSR is attempting to expand its shore-based infrastructure, particularly in Iraq, Aden, and India.[12]

12. See testimony by Director of the U.S. Central Intelligence Agency William E. Colby in *Congressional Record*, August 1, 1974, pp. 14092–93; and in *Allocation of Resources in the Soviet Union and China,* Hearings before the Subcommittee on Priorities and Economy in Government of the Joint Economic Committee, 93 Cong. 2 sess. (1974), pp. 32–33.

DRAFT INDIAN OCEAN NAVAL DISENGAGEMENT AGREEMENT

This draft illustrates the type of agreement mentioned in the text. Its substantive ideas are important but not its specific wording. In essence, this draft is intended to outline some of the issues that must be dealt with in any negotiation concerning naval disengagement. It is an attempt to indicate the concepts and does not purport to include all issues that may be material. In other words, it is a start.

The figures in parentheses are quantitative limitations that should be subjected to closer analysis. They indicate the order of magnitude to be considered, rather than a specific number of days, hours, boundary limits, and the like.

Brackets enclose items about which I am uncertain as to the most appropriate phraseology. All such items are discussed in the text.

Indian Ocean Naval Disengagement Agreement

I. Preamble

The Governments of the Union of the Soviet Socialist Republics and the United States of America, guided by the aims and principles of the United Nations as expressed in its Charter, declare their agreement that the basis of their policy in respect of the countries of the Indian Ocean region is the maintenance of peace in that region and in the whole world. Recognizing the need by way of negotiations for a peaceful settlement of all international problems and questions relating to the Indian Ocean region; and being aware of the importance of the responsibility which they carry for the maintenance of peace and security throughout the world, the Governments of the USSR and the United States agree to the following measures of naval disengagement.

II. Agreed Measures

1. Both parties agree to remove all [naval forces -or- warships and submarines] from the Indian Ocean within (30 days) of the ratification of this agreement, and to refrain from sending such forces into these areas during the duration of this agreement, except under the conditions described in subparagraphs a, b, c, d, and e.

a. Their respective [naval forces -or- warships and submarines] will only enter the Indian Ocean for one of the following reasons: to transit to another region, to make port visits on ceremonial occasions, to conduct training cruises, or to protect the lives of their nationals in emergency situations.

b. Each deployment of a [naval vessel -or- warship and submarine] to the Indian Ocean for one of the first three reasons listed in Section II, paragraph 1a, will be reported to the Joint Control Commission (JCC), described in Section III, at least (14 days) prior to entry; at no time will the [tonnage displaced at full load -and/or- number of vessels] deployed for these reasons exceed (?); and at no time will such vessels remain in the region for longer than (10 days), unless disabled and reported as such to the JCC.

c. Any deployment for reason of emergency will be reported to the JCC at least (24 hours) before entry, and the party not making the emergency deployment will have the right to match the [tonnage -and/or- number of] vessels being so deployed, so long as the emergency continues.

d. Reports of planned deployments into the Indian Ocean for any reasons listed above will include the following information: name and hull number, type designation and tonnage, entrance point and destination, course and milestones.

e. Any deviation from the reported deployment will be considered a violation of this agreement.

2. Both parties agree to eliminate all shore installations related to the support of their naval forces and located on islands in, or in nations on the littoral of, the Indian Ocean, and to refrain from the establishment of such bases for the duration of this agreement.

3. They are to renounce any existing agreements for the supply, repair, replenishment, or other form of support for naval forces with

Indian Ocean littoral nations, and to refrain from the conclusion of such arrangements for the duration of this agreement.

4. They agree to deposit, at the time of the ratification of this agreement, a list of such existing bases and agreements with the JCC, together with a schedule for their elimination.

5. [They agree to remove all other military forces and to eliminate all installations supporting such forces from nations bordering on the Indian Ocean, and to refrain from the establishment of such bases or the sending of such forces for the duration of this agreement. "Military forces" are defined to include all military personnel, with the exception ⋅ of defense attachés and technical advisers sent in connection with military equipment sales or aid programs but not to exceed (500) men in any one nation.]

III. Consultative Body

In order to implement and monitor this agreement, the Governments of the USSR and the United States agree to establish an organization known as the Joint Control Commission (JCC), consisting of a representative of each government [and one delegate nominated by the nations situated on the Indian Ocean littoral].

1. The JCC will meet to receive reports of [naval vessel or warship or submarine] deployments within (12 hours) of an emergency request and (3 days) of a normal request.

2. The JCC shall have a staff, composed of nationals of the contracting parties and of the littoral nations, of a size and composition as shall be determined by the JCC. This staff shall monitor naval activity in the Indian Ocean in a manner to be worked out by the JCC in conjunction with the littoral nations.

3. The JCC shall issue periodic reports as it deems advisable and establish its own rules of operation and procedure.

IV. Definition

For purposes of this agreement, the Indian Ocean is defined as follows:

a. The dividing line between the Atlantic and Indian Oceans is the meridian of Cape Agulhas (20°0′ east latitude).

b. The dividing line between the Pacific and Indian Oceans is the meridian of the South-East Cape of Tasmania (147°0′ east latitude), the western exit of the Bass Strait and the median line between Northwest Australia and the peninsula of Malay (the Cape of Talbot through Timor, Sumba, Flores and Sunda Islands, up to Sumatra).

c. The dividing line between the Antarctic Ocean and the Indian Ocean is the 60°0′ south latitude.

d. The northern limits are defined by the bordering land areas, and the Indian Ocean shall be considered to include bodies of water adjoining it on the north, such as the Red Sea, the Persian Gulf, the Arabian Sea, and the Bay of Bengal.

V. Duration

This agreement shall continue in effect for a period of (ten years) and be automatically renewed at that time for an additional (ten-year) period, unless one of the contracting parties objects. Either of the contracting parties may withdraw from this agreement (six months) following notice of such intent, if it deems such action necessary to its primary national interests. The agreement may be amended at any time upon approval of the representatives of both contracting parties in the JCC and contingent upon ratification by the respective parties according to their constitutional processes.

The agreement shall be considered null and void whenever a provision of Section II has been violated, or when an emergency deployment has been continued for longer than (thirty days).